Praise for *Why Kerouac Matters* by John Leland

"A head-snapper and a groundbreaker . . . By casting himself as the irreverent outsider, Leland gets farther inside the book, and inside the man, than Kerouac's solemn and sentimental partisans. . . . He reveals an intricacy and coherence hidden to those who approach Kerouac as a knuckle-dragger who got lucky."

—David Gates, *Newsweek*

"A fresh look at a classic road story . . . It's to the credit of Leland that he is able to bring a radically fresh perspective despite the cottage industry that the genesis of *On the Road* has become."

—*The Miami Herald*

"An intriguing, unconventional look at Kerouac, reading his classic novel less as an account of counterculture rebels than as a keynote into the mind of an author who held far more traditional views than many have imagined."

—*Rocky Mountain News*

"An entertaining and insightful book that supplies fresh observations on this much written about novel . . . It is about what *On the Road* can do for readers. . . . Leland delivers the goods page after page. . . . Over and over, Leland showed me something new and just as important, something fun."

—*The American Book Review*

"Leland makes a convincing case that *On the Road* is in many ways influenced by quest tales and religious allegories. That's just one of the several fresh ways of thinking about *On the Road* that Leland explores. . . . [*Why Kerouac Matters*] tickles our curiosity about a book and a writer we thought we knew, enticing us to take another look, go down another road."

—*The San Diego Union-Tribune*

"Fascinating . . . Trying to undo fifty . . . . ption about this twentieth-century mast . . . the mythology about Kerouac is a . . . to it with verve, wit, and a will . . . comparisons, asides, provocations . . . restrictive nicety in discussing Kerouac's classi . . . comparisons with hip-hop culture alongside the expecte . . .

and Whitmans. It has the effect of brushing away cobwebs or blowing the dust away to reveal new meanings. . . . The mystery and spirituality of Kerouac's most recognizable work is enhanced by Leland's serious and up to the minute appraisal." —*Beat Scene*

"Leland's book is insightful and offers a valuable corrective to the stereotypes that have clouded our vision of this seminal author."
—*The Weekly Standard*

"[Leland] explores some new paths in Kerouac studies. . . . [His] book is just as much about how to read a book well and deeply as it is about Kerouac. He avoids most scholarly and theoretical baggage but brings an inquisitive reader's intelligence to the table." —*The Kansas City Star*

"The most thought provoking of the new books [on Kerouac] is John Leland's *Why Kerouac Matters*. . . . True to the spontaneous, free-associational prose of its subject, the book is not just for Kerouaciacs, but well worth the time and attention of anyone interested in the man, his era, and his legacy."
—*The Washington Times*

"[A] sometimes arch, always discerning, and occasionally full-out brilliant reconsideration of a novel loved and maligned for all the wrong reasons. . . . As Leland shrewdly explicates the novel's spiritual teaching within dynamic social commentary, he links Kerouac to such antithetical realms as the Christian right and hip-hop, boldly recalibrating our understanding of an artist as immensely conflicted as we was gifted." —*ALA Booklist*

"Fantastic. Best writing about *On the Road*, and Kerouac, in fifty years." —Dave Moore

PENGUIN BOOKS

WHY KEROUAC MATTERS

John Leland is a reporter for *The New York Times*. He is the author of *Hip: The History*. He lives in New York City.

why KEROUAC matters

THE LESSONS OF *ON THE ROAD*

(they're not what you think)

JOHN LELAND

PENGUIN BOOKS

PENGUIN BOOKS

Published by the Penguin Group
Penguin Group (USA) Inc., 375 Hudson Street, New York, New York 10014, U.S.A.
Penguin Group (Canada), 90 Eglinton Avenue East, Suite 700, Toronto, Ontario, Canada M4P
2Y3 (a division of Pearson Penguin Canada Inc.) • Penguin Books Ltd, 80 Strand, London
WC2R 0RL, England • Penguin Ireland, 25 St Stephen's Green, Dublin 2, Ireland (a division of
Penguin Books Ltd) • Penguin Group (Australia), 250 Camberwell Road, Camberwell, Victoria
3124, Australia (a division of Pearson Australia Group Pty Ltd) • Penguin Books India Pvt Ltd,
11 Community Centre, Panchsheel Park, New Delhi – 110 017, India • Penguin Group (NZ),
67 Apollo Drive, Rosedale, North Shore 0632, New Zealand (a division of Pearson New Zealand
Ltd) • Penguin Books (South Africa) (Pty) Ltd, 24 Sturdee Avenue, Rosebank, Johannesburg
2196, South Africa

Penguin Books Ltd, Registered Offices: 80 Strand, London WC2R 0RL, England

First published in the United States of America by Viking Penguin,
a member of Penguin Group (USA) Inc. 2007
Published in Penguin Books 2008

10 9 8 7 6 5 4 3 2 1

Grateful acknowledgment is made for permission to reprint excerpts from the following
copyrighted works:
  On the Road by Jack Kerouac. Copyright © John Sampas, Literary Representative, the Estate of
Stella Sampas Kerouac; John Lash, Executor of the Estate of Jan Kerouac; Nancy Bump; and
Anthony M. Sampas, 1955, 1957. Used by permission of Viking Penguin, a member of Penguin
Group (USA) Inc.
  Selected Letters (Volumes 1 and 2) by Jack Kerouac, edited by Ann Charters (Viking). Copyright
© the Estate of Stella Kerouac, John Sampas, Literary Representative, 1995, 1999. By permission
of John Sampas, Executor, the Estate of Stella Sampas Kerouac.
  Windblown World: The Journals of Jack Kerouac 1947–1954, edited by Douglas Brinkley. Copyright
© the Estate of Stella Kerouac, John Sampas, Literary Representative, 2004. Used by permission
of Viking Penguin, a member of Penguin Group (USA) Inc.

THE LIBRARY OF CONGRESS HAS CATALOGED THE HARDCOVER EDITION AS FOLLOWS:
Leland, John, 1959–
Why Kerouac matters : the lessons of On the road (they're not what you think) / John Leland.
p. cm.
Includes bibliographical references.
ISBN 978-0-670-06325-3 (hc.)
ISBN 978-0-14-311437-6 (pbk.)
1. Kerouac, Jack, 1922–1969. On the road.   2. Autobiographical fiction, American—History
and criticism.   3. Beat generation in literature.   I. Title.
PS3521.E735O5347   2007
813'.54—dc22   2007006040

Printed in the United States of America
Designed by Carla Bolte • Set in Iowan

FOR ROBERT P. LELAND, 1921–2004

The fact of the matter is, I'm not a bestseller because people aren't educated enough yet: just wait and see what the Astronauts of the Year 2,000 B.C. [sic] will be reading on Venus and Mars ('t'wont be James Michener).

—Letter to Stella Sampas, 1965

[I] don't know how to drive, just typewrite.

—Letter to Neal Cassady, 1953

CONTENTS

Visions of Sal: The Book of Revelations

The Aftermath: Success and Its Discontents

why

KEROUAC

matters

Girls, Visions, Everything

THE EDUCATION OF SAL PARADISE

Growing Up Kerouac

The Parable of the Wet Hitchhiker

What Would Jack Do?

Who are you indeed who would talk or sing to America?
Have you studied out the land, its idioms and men?

—Walt Whitman, "By Blue Ontario's Shore"

I'll have seen 41 states in all. Is that enough for an American
novelist?

—Kerouac, letter to sister, Caroline (Nin), 1947

IN October 1948, Jack Kerouac wrote to his friend Hal
Chase that he had started a new novel, an "American-scene
picaresque" about two boys hitchhiking to California, one for a
girl, the other for Hollywood stardust. The characters would
work crap jobs across the country, "arriving finally in California
where there is nothing" and return home. The idea for the book
obsessed him, he told Chase; it burst out of him in bars among
strangers and in letters to friends across town.

Over the next two and a half years, he started and stopped
the book, testing out different characters and situations. He tried
Red Moultrie, a former minor-league outfielder and sometime
safecracker; Warren Beauchamp, raised on a California ranch;
Ray Smith, a hipster Boswell with natty clothes; Vern Pomeroy,
a motherless child seeking his hobo father. Their early adventures included a stoner "tea party" and a pulpy jail episode
among cons named "Yogi and the Hook, and Big Czech and
Rocco and all the gunmen of Blood Inc." One draft began with a
supplication to God, like a prayer or a Homeric epic.

But Kerouac held constant about what the book should do. "[M]y writing is a teaching," he noted in his journal, and this was the point, even if readers didn't get it at first. "One of the greatest incentives of the writer is the long business of getting his teachings out and accepted." He was twenty-six when he started composing the novel, shaking off a brief failed marriage and the death of his father, embarking on the next phase of his life. The new book would teach the way. To prepare, he wrote down eleven "true thoughts" about himself, many of them vanities he hoped to overcome along his characters' travels. "I'm ready to grow up if they'll let me," he wrote. The product of his labors, he was sure, would be a "powerful and singularly gloomy book . . . but good."

The book, of course, is *On the Road*, its title punning on Neal Cassady's phrase for being high—"gone on the road." By the time he sat down in April 1951 and speed-typed the tale on a 120-foot scroll of taped-together tracing paper, the characters had become Jack and Neal—under their real names—and the hoosegow and Big Czech were discarded, along with any natty haberdashery. The longest hitchhiking stretch ran only from Chicago to Denver. But the teaching imperative remained. Beneath its wild yea-saying, *On the Road* is a book about how to live your life.

Its form is simple and episodic, charting a friendship across five journeys, from winter 1947 to January 1951. Though the material came from Kerouac's real life, he worked it with the license of a novelist. It took six years to get the manuscript published, making Kerouac a thirty-five-year-old boy wonder whose life was far from the one readers imagined: living mostly at his mother's house, broke, working away at manuscripts that no one wanted to publish. When the book finally came out, on September 5,

1957, with the characters' names changed for legal reasons, the success and attendant controversies all but destroyed him.

In the half century since its publication, *On the Road* has echoed anew through successive rebel youth movements, from the sixties counterculture to the alternative tribes of the post-9/11 era. "Woodstock rises from his pages," wrote Kerouac's friend William Burroughs, who appears as Bull Lee in the book. Bob Dylan said he cherished it "like a Bible" in his youth. Johnny Depp paid $15,000 for Kerouac's old raincoat, and Jim Irsay, owner of the Indianapolis Colts, paid $2.43 million for the original scroll manuscript. Even among writers, it is not so much a literary model as a personal code. "There are two kinds of things guys like us do," said Michael Herr, author of the Vietnam journal *Dispatches*, speaking to the novelist Robert Stone. "The things we do because we read Jack Kerouac and the things we do because we read Hemingway." If you want to spot a rebel in a movie or television show, look for a copy of *On the Road* on his bookshelf.

But viewing the book through this filter provides a distorted picture, reflecting only what the marketplace has blessed over the years. Economists call this tendency "survivorship bias." If Woodstock was a populist celebration of rebellion, according to the bias, then Kerouac must be a populist and a rebel. If he is a hero to adolescents, he must be an adolescent hero. Yet Kerouac was none of those things, and his intention for *On the Road* was not to promote Woodstock or rebellion any more than it was to sell Dockers. He had only regrets for the sectarian furies of youth culture, which he saw as divisive and negative. "Woe unto those . . . who believe in hating mothers and fathers, who deny the most important of the Ten Commandments," he admonished. "[W]oe unto those who believe in conflict and horror and violence and fill our books and screens and livingrooms with all that crap." His book contains twenty-three references to "kicks," but as many to God or Jesus.

What has thrived in the market, in fact, is not Kerouac but Dean Moriarty, the fast-talking, mad-driving philosopher who initiates the narrator in the ways of the road. The Book of Dean is one of the most compelling rides in American literature, a perfect pop song: sexy, sideburned, hypnotic, all-consuming and consumed in an instant. It has a good beat and you can dance to it. But it is not the whole of *On the Road*.

John Clellon Holmes, whose 1952 *Go* is considered the first Beat novel, recalled that even people who met Kerouac confused him with his fellow traveler, at great cost to the author. Strangers expected him to be a walking party. "They weren't looking in the right place," Holmes said; "they weren't looking at the work; they were looking at their image of the man, an image which they derived from the few works which they had read. They kept mixing Jack up with Dean Moriarty, in other words with Neal Cassady. They kept thinking he was Dean Moriarty but he wasn't."

Finding Paradise

So a first step in excavating *On the Road* is to separate Kerouac from Cassady, and Sal Paradise, the first-person narrator, from Dean Moriarty. This separation is not always easy, even for the characters. When Sal tries to put a little space between them in the book, leaving Dean behind in New York, Dean's specter comes rampaging in pursuit: "a burning shuddering frightful Angel, palpitating toward me across the road, approaching like a cloud, with enormous speed, pursuing me like the Shrouded

Traveler on the plain, bearing down on me. I saw his huge face over the plains with the mad, bony purpose and the gleaming eyes; I saw his wings; I saw his old jalopy chariot with thousands of sparking flames shooting out from it; I saw the path it burned over the road; it even made its own road and went over the corn, through cities, destroying bridges, drying rivers. It came like wrath to the West. I knew Dean had gone mad again."

Sal's book, then, is not Dean's. If Dean is a pop single, Sal, like Kerouac, is the evolving opera: somber, God-pondering, watchful, confessional, given to teaching and learning. "What gloom!" Sal says after seeing Beethoven's *Fidelio* in Colorado, echoing the baritone's dungeon aria. "I cried for it. That's how I see life too." Dean spends the book racing away from the messes he makes of his life, while Sal tries to figure out how to live amid the mess handed him. Dean has his reasons for hitting the road— he is *all* reasons—but, like the reasons in a pop song, they are not the point. We all know the reasons for hitting the road. Sal's reasons are those of a novel, to be developed over the course of the work, not in advance of it.

In a postwar culture that was discovering the magic of adolescence, the novel wrestles openly with the issue of how to grow up—how to *adolesce*. The question ultimately divides the two main characters. From Sal's opening journey west, when he lives on a child's diet of ice cream and apple pie, he crosses "the dividing line between the East of my youth and the West of my future," knowing that the experience will change him. Dean, on the other hand, arrives in the novel fully formed, "the perfect guy for the road because he actually was born on the road." His travels can only bring him toward a more childlike state, innocent of the wreckage he causes—blameless, an Angel, the Holy

Goof. For Sal alone the road is a path of growth. As long as Dean remains a child, tempting Sal to do the same, Sal's maturation can be a free choice, not a concession to social expectations or simply a product of age.

You might say, "Wait a minute, Kerouac didn't mature, he sunk deeper into drink, insecurity and his mother's toxic bosom." But that's reading *On the Road* as a memoir, not a work of fiction.

The Five Journeys

- July to October 1947: Sal joins Dean briefly in Denver, leaves by bus to San Francisco and back to New York.

- Christmas 1948: Dean picks up Sal in a Hudson roadster. With Ed Dunkel and Marylou, they visit Bull Lee in Louisiana, then continue to San Francisco. Sal takes the bus home.

- Spring 1949: Sal goes to Denver to find a home, gets bored, goes to Dean in San Francisco. They drive crazy travel-bureau cars back to New York.

- Spring 1950: Sal leaves Dean in New York, goes to Denver. Dean follows, wraithlike. With Stan Shephard, they drive to Mexico City, where Dean leaves Sal with dysentery.

- January 1951: Dean comes to New York, Sal abandons him for limo to Duke Ellington concert.

Like any novelist, Kerouac constructed his story selectively, emphasizing or omitting details to develop themes, messing with time and character. "You're not really writing a book till you begin to *take liberties* with it," he wrote in his journal in 1949. "I've begun to do this with On the Road now." He ends with Sal sober, at peace, ensconced in domestic life with a new flame named Laura, a great beauty who offers him cocoa and a home in her loft. Kerouac's friends, on reading the manuscript, thought it lacked an ending, perhaps because the resolution was so far from Kerouac's life. But Kerouac stuck with his ending through years of revisions, even as the loft and the life there receded to a brief, bitter memory. Novels are, among other things, expressions of faith in endings.

This faith leads Sal first toward Dean as a mentor and a liberator, then past him, until his final view of Dean is from the backseat of a Cadillac, with Dean standing on a cold New York street, "ragged in a motheaten overcoat," and Sal warm inside with Laura, on their way to a Duke Ellington concert at the Metropolitan Opera House. Earlier Sal had asked, "What is that feeling when you're driving away from people and they recede on the plain till you see their specks dispersing?" and had answered his own question—"it's the too-huge world vaulting us, and it's good-by. But we lean forward to the next crazy venture beneath the skies." On these journeys Sal hopes to be judged as an adult, for what he *produces*, his writing; Dean will be judged as a child, for what he *is*. In due course Sal learns and dispenses many lessons, often in the form of parables and revelations, providing a guide to alternative adulthood: What Would Jack Do? Contrary to its rebel rep, *On the Road* is not about being Peter Pan; it is about becoming an adult. Its story is powerful and singularly gloomy . . . but good.

When it was published, in 1957, the best-selling novel in America was Grace Metalious's *Peyton Place*, a saucy indictment of mill-town American values. Her success followed Sloan Wilson's equally of-its-day *The Man in the Gray Flannel Suit*, an indictment of suburban values and the rat race. Both books far outsold *On the Road* at the time, and both were made into successful movies. Yet nobody reads them today, and the movies endure mainly as kitsch. *On the Road* has remained a rite of passage because it is not an indictment of its times but an affirmative response. It survives because, like *The Road Less Traveled* or *The Purpose Driven Life*, it gives readers something they can use.

Sal's lessons divide among four overlapping fields, each unsettled in the postwar boom. America had emerged from the war with half the world's wealth and nearly two thirds of its machines, and with destructive capacities unmatched in history. It was creating suburbs, television, organization men, nuclear families, the car culture, Brando, McCarthy and rock and roll. Amid this tumult, Sal navigates distinct paths through the men's world of work, money and friendship; the domestic turf of love, sex and family; the artist's realm of storytelling, improvisation and rhythm; and the spiritual world of revelation and redemption. His lessons in all four areas remain relevant today—any reader picking up the book for the first time can apply them to questions that are as new to him or her as they were to Sal.

His lessons begin, appropriately, at the start of the road, with the book's first parable.

[T]he things I write are what an editor usually throws away and what a psychiatrist finds most interesting.

—Remark to *The San Francisco Examiner*, 1957

FOR his first journey on the road, Sal rides the Seventh Avenue subway up to 242nd Street in the Bronx, the end of the line, then travels beside the Hudson River up to Bear Mountain. For months he'd studied books and maps of the West, enchanted by names like Platte and Cimarron and by legends of the pioneers. His plan is to hitchhike along the red line of Route 6 from Bear Mountain clear to Los Angeles, a single ribbon connecting sea to sea. In his imagination he'd practically seen the land unbuttoning. Now he is at the starting point and there is not a ride in sight. Rain mocks his wet huaraches; thunderclaps shake the hairy mountain. "[T]here's no traffic passes through Route 6," a man at a filling station tells him. Forty miles from home, and already his plans have led him astray.

Somewhere along the line, he believed, "there'd be girls, visions, everything; somewhere along the line the pearl would be handed to me." But for now there is only a man telling him to take the bus toward Pittsburgh.

So the road begins not in kicks but in failure, with the book's first lesson: He must leave behind the boyish certainties of books and learn to improvise, play the changes—diversify. "It was my dream that screwed up," he realizes, "the stupid hearthside idea that it would be wonderful to follow one great red line across America instead of trying various roads and routes." Even on this first journey he is after something: not just freedom and escape, which he has without asking, but their opposites, faith and engagement. Raised in the Catholic Church and steeped in the American romance of Walt Whitman, he's on a quest, not a breakout or a mutiny. Sal wants to belong.

Kerouac spelled out this vision of the road in an unmailed letter to Hal Chase in 1947. Conceding his poor track record at domestic life, he wrote of his wanderlust, "I know some people who would regard it as a kind of recidivous childishness. And yet I know some people who would regard it as a step ahead . . . a purposeful energetic search after useful knowledge." He saw himself following in the path of Mark Twain, producing significant work while living in a "vast and significant way." Above all, he reminded himself, "heroism is still my goal."

In its parables and meditations, the road offers Sal a way around the decidedly unheroic battles fought in *Peyton Place* and *The Man in the Gray Flannel Suit*. He wants to become a man, but not like the examples of manhood that surround him. "This is the story of America," Sal laments at one point, finding himself among complacent workers. "Everybody's doing what they think they're supposed to do." We've become accustomed to describing such discontent as rebellion, in part because the market loves rebellion, but Sal does not really rebel. He just moves on, navigating through the adult male specimens without making them his problem: the corporate drone, the fat phony businessman, the persnickety intellectual naysayers of New York. It is a neat literary sidestep, often unremarked. These grown men are all somehow infantilized, stunted short of authentic maturity. Their roads are not for Sal—nor, finally, is Dean's serial profligacy.

The Parable of the Wet Hitchhiker is the first step in his maturation. On its surface, it is an attempt by Sal to be like his friend. Dean has just blown into town, captivated everyone with his manic energy and pendulous sexuality, and blown out again. "I promised myself to go the same way," Sal says, watching "our wrangler" disappear into the West. Dean enters the novel like a happy virus, infecting everyone in his path. (Cassady's visit had a literal epidemiology as well, according to Kerouac's biographer Gerald Nicosia—he gave everyone crabs, "one of the less literary influences of Neal Cassady.")

In these opening scenes, Sal echoes the restlessness of another vagabond narrator, Ishmael, from *Moby-Dick*. Melville, who had fallen into obscurity before his death in 1891, was rediscovered by the Greenwich Village bohemians of the twenties and by Kerouac's time was required reading for hipsters. Kerouac felt a special kinship. His own first, unpublished novel, *The Sea Is My Brother*, recounted his days as a scullion in the merchant marine, and he likened *On the Road*'s form to "Melville of Confidence Man & parts of Moby Dick." In the scroll draft, the narrator calls himself "a veritable Ishmael" heading out on his first journey.

So it is worth revisiting Ishmael's opening lines: "Whenever I find myself growing grim about the mouth; whenever it is a damp, drizzly November in my soul; whenever I find myself involuntarily pausing before coffin warehouses, and bringing up the rear of every funeral I meet; and especially whenever my hypos get such an upper hand of me, that it requires a strong moral principle to prevent me from deliberately stepping into the street, and methodically knocking people's hats off—then, I account it high time to get to sea as soon as I can. This is my substitute for pistol and ball. With a philosophical flourish Cato throws himself upon his sword; I quietly take to the ship."

Like Melville's Captain Ahab, Dean will prove a destructive leader, and the road a trial, not a joyful escape. Both narrators know what they're getting into. As Ishmael says, following Ahab, "I gave myself up to the abandonment of the time and the place; and while yet all a-rush to encounter the whale, could see naught in that brute but the deadliest ill." Sal refers to Dean explicitly as "that mad Ahab at the wheel" and the road as a ribbon of sea. Sal will have to learn to keep Dean at a distance or suffer the white whale—another myth that proved beautiful but ruinous.

Sal repeats the mistake of the Wet Hitchhiker throughout his first journey, reading people and experiences through his preconceptions. He sees archetypes, not persons. Dean, for example, is a movie poster, "a young Gene Autry—trim, thin-hipped, blue-eyed, with a real Oklahoma accent—a sideburned hero of the snowy West." Sal's experiences on this journey are accordingly ersatz. Drawn by his bookish illusion of the West, he finds exactly that, landing in Cheyenne, Wyoming, in the middle of Wild West Week, amid "big crowds of businessmen, fat businessmen in boots and ten-gallon hats, with their hefty wives in cowgirl attire. . . . [I]n my first shot at the West I was seeing to what absurd devices it had fallen to keep its proud tradition." So he is only partially on the road, still attached to the dreamy notions he formed before leaving home.

Until he gives them up, he is forever bound to repeat his mistakes. When he picks up a Mexican girl named Terry on a bus to

Los Angeles, he imagines their meeting as the scene from Preston Sturges's film *Sullivan's Travels* where Joel McCrea meets Veronica Lake in a diner. This is a tip-off to the lesson Sal finds in the affair. McCrea's character, a pampered Hollywood director, immerses himself among poor workers as research for a social-realist movie called *O Brother, Where Art Thou?*, only to realize that poor people don't want this sentimental voyeurism. Sal, too, is lost in a romantic myth of poverty. He describes Terry's skin as "brown as grapes," which makes no sense except as a flag to readers that he sees her as a stereotype of a Mexican-American grape picker, not a person. Their romance, like the whole of the first journey, proceeds as a series of false identifications. He thinks she's a prostitute; she thinks he's a college boy, then a pimp. Like Sullivan, he enters other people's worlds only on his own terms, which prevents him from seeing anything else.

His illusions lead him to the book's most ill-advised passage, when he is working beside Terry in a California cotton field and sees an elderly African-American couple. "They picked cotton with the same God-blessed patience their grandfathers had practiced in ante-bellum Alabama," he writes, and we should not feel proud that we know better today. Though Kerouac has been justly criticized for this line, it is consistent with the blindness and naïveté Sal shows throughout the first journey, since the Parable of the Wet Hitchhiker. He pays a price for his blindness—he is denied the gift of prophecy. Coming into Denver from Cheyenne, he imagines himself in his friends' eyes, "strange and ragged like the Prophet who has walked across the land to bring the dark Word, and the only Word I had was 'Wow!'" As a writer whose role it is to deliver the Word, he is not ready. It will take several trips and further parables before he acquires this gift.

When he finally abandons the journey and returns to "the pull of my own life," he gets a glimpse of the reality behind the illusion. As he waits for the eastbound bus from Los Angeles, preparing sandwiches that won't last the journey, great klieg lights of a Hollywood premiere slice the sky, reminding him that his own movie script has won him nothing but rejection. "All around me were the noises of the crazy gold-coast city," he says. "And this was my Hollywood career—this was my last night in Hollywood, and I was spreading mustard on my lap in back of a parking-lot john."

His encounters with myth on this journey are part of Sal's education in the postwar landscape. *On the Road* arrived just as the new medium of television was colonizing American consciousness with its own fables and archetypes, further entangling truth and image. TV creates its own geography, bringing the far near and the outdoors indoors. Exploring this new America means, in part, navigating media images and mythologies as well as highways and mountains. As Sal moves horizontally around the country, he moves vertically through the America of Hollywood, Wild West Week, Whitman, *Huckleberry Finn*, *Moby-Dick*, bebop and his own romantic imagination.

The media turned Kerouac into an instant national celebrity, the dreaded "voice of a generation," and wrapped his book in a swashbuckling public image that was as illusory as any of Sal's starry preconceptions. As if in anticipation, there is an implicit message throughout the book's first trip not to take myths for revelations. The road, Dean, the West, Hollywood, the ideal family—all will prove other than what Sal imagines.

Bringing the Dark Word

In May 1961, Kerouac received a letter from a theology student named Carroll Brown asking about the themes of *On the Road*. By then Kerouac's life was a drunken mess, and the literary respect he'd belatedly won with *On the Road* was already in decline. Despite good reviews for his first published novel, *The Town and the City*, in 1950, no publisher wanted *On the Road* when he started shopping it in 1951. By the time the Viking Press issued it in September 1957, Kerouac had written a dozen more books, all without a publisher. "I just keep turning out manuscripts like a machine and they just keep flying away into the void," he wrote to his agent, Sterling Lord. "[W]hat other writer can keep this up and not go crazy like I'm about to do?"

To Brown's question he wrote a thoughtful (if tardy) reply, pointing out that there was no violence in *On the Road*—he didn't count Dean's violence against women—and none of the hooliganism for which the book was regularly blamed. The themes, he wrote, were spiritual. "Dean and I were embarked on a tremendous journey through post-Whitman America to FIND that America and to FIND the inherent goodness in American man," he explained. "It was really a story about 2 Catholic buddies roaming the country in search of God. And we found him."

This unhip story of a search for God and human goodness has eluded most readers. America has a tradition of sad singers whose pain is consumed as freedom or joy, going back at least to Mark Twain, the nation's greatest humorist, who lived with a broken heart and a merry white suit. Kerouac and his gloomy narrator join a fellowship of dolor that includes Twain, Bert Williams, W. C. Fields, F. Scott Fitzgerald, Dorothy Parker, Charlie

Parker, Jackson Pollock, Richard Pryor, Tupac Shakur and Kurt Cobain, to name only a few. All became masters of ceremony for catharses they could not share. There is nothing more sorrowful than the laughter at a W. C. Fields movie, unless it is the hormonal "Hell yeah!" at a Nirvana concert. That Kerouac, who lived with his mother, became an icon of youth rebellion was an irony he could not accept, but it was an irony as American as he was. There is a reason America is the home of the blues.

Sal's Blues

On the Road begins in 1947 in a key of loss. "I first met Neal not long after my father died," Kerouac opened his 1951 scroll draft. "I had just gotten over a serious illness that I won't bother to talk about except that it really had something to do with my father's death and my feeling that everything was dead." Kerouac once described a great bop pianist "dropping huge chords like a Wolfean horse turding in the steamy Brooklyn winter morn." This opening line is such a chord. In the published version, he changed his father's death to the "miserably weary" split-up of his first marriage, but the mournfulness remained. *Is this the line that launched a thousand kicks?* This blues refrain came organically to Sal; it was how Kerouac saw the world. In notes for the book, he mused, "Where are we all? Gone on the road. . . . What's at the end? Night . . . whatever Celine meant by giving death that name, whatever kind of death he meant." Kerouac felt he was being punished by God and that the writer's role was to do penance for the world's sins. His punishment was to experience the world and "labor great books."

Kerouac's Catholicism underlies the characters' quest in *On the Road*. "I forgot to mention," he wrote later, "that we were both devout little Catholics in our childhood, which gives us something in common tho we never talk about it." Raised in the blue-collar, French-Canadian Catholic Church in Lowell, Massachusetts, he drifted away in his teens and as an adult discovered and eventually discarded Buddhism, settling finally on a home-grown form of mystic Catholicism. But he held always to the mysterious and gnostic, and to a prophet's sense of time, which articulates the past within the fallen present.

The challenge for his novel, then, was to repair a breach in post-Whitman America and find the goodness within it. Like Whitman, Kerouac sang for the land and its flawed people—multitudinous like himself, filled with potential and contradiction. The narrator's name is a not-so-subtle clue to this intention: He is Salvatore and his road is to Paradise. (Dean is Moriarty, the brilliant adversary.) Kerouac felt that the country had betrayed its great promise, starting "when fools left the covered wagons in 1848 and rode madly to California for Gold, leaving their families behind."

Sal's offering will be in revelation, aiming not to fix America's problems but to expiate them. American man was good but fallen; he needed forgiveness and atonement, not rational analysis or reform. *"Issues,"* Kerouac would say. *"Fuck issues."* He wasn't interested in progressive reforms because, as he told his friend Ed White, they were like the problems they were meant to fix, just another kind of materialism. "It will all fall apart like Rome if there isn't a renaissance in American feeling," he told White. "Our modern art depicting life-dissatisfaction certainly isn't helping."

When Sal receives his calling late in the novel, it is to take up this prophetic duty. "I heard the sound of footsteps from the darkness beyond, and lo, a tall old man with flowing white hair came clomping by with a pack on his back, and when he saw me as he passed, he said, '*Go moan for man,*' and clomped on back to his dark." Charged with this commission, Sal writes the book we read today. Go moan for man, man.

Sal's visionary experiences give shape to the book's journeys. In a 1951 letter to Cassady, which Kerouac worked into the novel, he described a vision he had in San Francisco when he was broke and hungry and abandoned. Peering into the window of a fish-and-chips joint, he suddenly saw the owner as his mother from an earlier lifetime, looking angry that he had traveled across time to haunt her. "I stood completely stoned on the sidewalk in unbelievable and heavenly rapture," he wrote to Cassady. "For a moment like that I'd be willing to suffer a whole ten years of grimness again. . . . Because if I were ready for that vision, as I was not then, I think I would be able to understand everything and never forget it; particularly I think I would know the nature of God and all the life He made, and I would be so saved nobody could find me any more."

But of course he couldn't comprehend the nature of God or re-create it with words. In the novel's version of the scene, Sal again approaches understanding but falls short. Seeing the vision from his past life, he says, "for just a moment I had reached the point of ecstasy that I always wanted to reach, which was the complete step across chronological time into timeless shadows, and wonderment in the bleakness of the mortal realm, and the sensation of death kicking at my heels to move on, with a phantom dogging its own heels, and myself hurrying to a plank where all the angels dove off and flew into the holy void of uncreated emptiness, the potent and inconceivable radiancies shining in bright Mind Essence. . . . I was too young to know what had happened."

By the time Sal tells this story, he is no longer so young. But he is still unable to know the nature of God or, if he knew it, to pass it along as a plot point in a novel. He could only blur the image enough to let the nonrational in. As to the supernatural element, it is up to readers to receive it musically, as a blues listener receives a whole spectrum of meaning in a slurred note. This is a challenge of *On the Road*, and another reason it is easier to read it as Dean's book rather than Sal's. Sal's book is a process of naming the unnamable.

For this he develops some rhetorical tools, including . . .

The Reverse Con

In real life, Neal Cassady's arrival in New York provoked mixed reactions. Allen Ginsberg and Kerouac were enthralled. Raised on Denver's skid row, the son of a hobo, able to quote Schopenhauer and steal cars, Cassady was a fantasy they couldn't act out themselves. He made Kerouac feel inauthentic, said Holmes, who knew both men later. "Neal was enormously attractive to people who sat on their ass most of the day in a dim room, biting their nails, and typing out shit." Others were less impressed. Ed White, who had known Cassady in Denver, thought he was a parasite and a phony. Tom Livornese, a friend who opened his apartment to Cassady and his child bride, LuAnne, found his rap "an astronomic con of the worst sort."

Hal Chase, who also knew Cassady from their Denver days, took a more pragmatic view. He had ridden with Cassady in stolen cars and was struck by his combination of energy and criminality. Chase encouraged him to come to New York, feeding Kerouac and Cassady each other's letters. To Chase, Cassady represented just what Kerouac needed: He was a perfect subject to write about.

The Reverse Con, like any good con, is a story that takes a

long time to develop. It builds on the Wet Hitchhiker's lesson with a more nuanced appreciation of bullshit—acknowledging the magic of myth without wholly stepping in it. Simply to renounce illusion would be to renounce Dean, the West, the road and the clarion call of Whitman's America. It is the dullest and most reductive form of secularism. If *On the Road* is a spiritual quest, it cannot love only the factual. Myth has truth, too: It delivers the truth of the past in the present. But you can't go around with stars in your eyes. The Reverse Con has it both ways.

It begins with a simple con. Dean, new in town, transparently sets to work on his new friends. He ingratiates himself to Sal by asking him to teach him to write and to Carlo Marx, the Ginsberg character, via more southerly latitudes. "Go ahead, everything you do is great," he tells Sal, who eats it up. Yet Sal is not entirely supine. In Dean's manipulations, Sal recognizes a fellow craftsman. "He was conning me and I knew it (for room and board and 'how-to-write,' etc.), and he knew I knew (this has been the basis of our relationship)." The con man is a storyteller, a writer; he creates a narrative in which listeners imagine themselves. Sal, who is learning to tell a story—not yet able to bring the dark Word—is working a con of his own. "Yes," he writes, "and it wasn't only because I was a writer and needed new experiences that I wanted to know Dean more."

A first-person narrative involves a special kind of con, because the narrator pretends to know less than he does. As he paces alongside the other characters, he alone knows how things will shake out. When we see Sal gazing on Dean for the first time, full of wonder, we are doing so through eyes that have already seen Dean in collapse or as the destructive wraith rampaging across the desert. Sal plays the most naïve character in the book, but he knows the most. He tips his hand in his opening description of Dean, characterizing him as "not the way he is today," a view of Dean at two points in time, reached only after the book's action is complete. So Sal is conning us as Dean is conning him.

The Reverse Con resides in the way Sal treats his oracular knowledge. Though Dean constantly raps at him, "We know time," it is actually Sal who knows time, because he can move back and forth in tense. While praising Dean, he casually mentions future betrayals, wising readers up to "Dean's eventual rejection of me as a buddy, putting me down, as he would later, on starving sidewalks and sickbeds." It is the middle phrase—"putting me down, as he would later"—that rubs hardest against the nature of their quest and the heroic portrait of Dean.

But what did it matter? Sal asks. "I was a young writer and I wanted to take off." Dean is the gasoline on these travels, not the destination. When Dean abandons him finally, leaving him in Mexico with dysentery, Sal cuts his friend with kindness. "When I got better I realized what a rat he was, but then I had to understand the impossible complexity of his life, how he had to leave me there, sick, to get on with his wives and his woes. 'Okay, old Dean, I'll say nothing.'" Dean's wives and woes, of course, are really further strikes against him. And if this is Sal's way of saying nothing, who needs a formal indictment?

This ability to see things in two states at the same time—to see Dean as both myth and rat, or Hollywood as hollow and resonant—is a model for Sal's lessons in storytelling and time. It underlies Kerouac's quest to find Whitman's America in the post-Whitman landscape. Like the book's structure, it employs a jazz way of knowledge, completing a chorus by improvising on it from every angle, with each version contributing to the whole.

Sal closes Part One by putting this knowledge to work in two parables of his possible future. These are . . .

The Parables of the Ghost and the Thin Man

On his return trip, hitchhiking east outside Harrisburg, Pennsylvania, he encounters an old man he calls the Ghost of the Susquehanna. The old vagabond is a bookend for the first journey—a projection of the Wet Hitchhiker into shriveled old age. Again the night is rainy, and the Ghost, like the Wet Hitchhiker, is going in the wrong direction. He is an apparition of what Sal might become, headed for "Canady" with no sense of how to get there or why. The encounter shows Sal where the Wet Hitchhiker's romantic folly leads, to a life without sinew or direction.

This time Sal sees his error and turns away from the Ghost, viewing him not as a romantic adventurer but a "little hobo standing under a sad streetlamp with his thumb stuck out—poor forlorn man, poor lost sometimeboy, now broken ghost of the penniless wilds." As Sal leaves the Ghost and rights his bearings, he hears a tenor man "blowing a very fine blues" from a hick roadhouse, an angel of the road, and for the first time in the book Sal "listened and moaned."

Yet Sal also sees the mythic in the Ghost's lost rambles, and refines his own myth of the frontier. "I thought all the wilderness of America was in the West till the Ghost of the Susquehanna showed me different. No, there is a wilderness in the East; it's the same wilderness Ben Franklin plodded in the oxcart days when he was postmaster, the same as it was when George Washington was a wildbuck Indian-fighter, when Daniel Boone told stories by Pennsylvania lamps and promised to find the Gap." The Ghost is a ghost because he inhabits the past and present simultaneously. This is the presence of Whitman's America in Sal's own, a near-complete step across chronological time. The American wilderness, which Sal sings throughout *On the Road*, is not a destination but a way of seeing.

When the rational and scientific make their return, in the person of Sal's ride to New York, they are literally a force of self-annihilation. The driver, a traveling salesman, is on a "controlled starvation" diet, which reduces him to "a bag of bones, a floppy doll, a broken stick, a maniac." His faith in science is killing him. For Sal, starved from his travels, the man is a parody of secular wisdom, reducing himself to nothing in the name of scientific progress. (Kerouac embraced asceticism as a path to revelation, not as a health kick.) Faced with these two visions of adulthood—one the result of too much romance, the other too much science—Sal does not want to mature into either. He will need to find another route.

He takes a first step away from his childhood security. "Isn't it true that you start your life a sweet child believing in everything under your father's roof?" he asks himself. "Then comes the day of the Laodiceans, when you know you are wretched and miserable and poor and blind and naked, and with the visage of a gruesome grieving ghost you go shuddering through nightmare life." The reference is to the book of Revelation, when Jesus commands John to chastise the Laodicean church for believing in its material wealth, and calls on members to recognize that they are "wretched, pitiable, poor, blind, and naked."

For Sal it means there will be great suffering and sacrifice on the way to enlightenment. His further travels begin with this understanding.

Science will not get him there, nor boyish fantasy, including the romance of Dean. Sal has left the certainties of his father's roof, and he has seen himself wretched, pitiable and poor. But he hasn't quite figured it out. When he reaches his aunt's house at the end of his first journey, to "figure the losses and figure the gain that I knew was in there somewhere too," they survey his torn cottonfield pants and tattered shoes—and decide to buy an electric refrigerator, like every other household of the time.

Yet he is on his way, with a budding sense of direction and purpose. On the way east, a girl had bought him a meal in exchange for his long stories. This is the start of his productive labors. With eyes salved, he writes, "It was October, home, and work again."

[G]o home, go marry yr. love, another winter's come and catching you.

—Notes for early draft of *On the Road*, July 1950

IN May 1950, Kerouac grilled himself in his journal about why he traveled so much. He had been at *On the Road* for more than a year and a half, producing many dead ends but also passages that he used in the 1951 scroll draft and ultimately in the version we know. *The Town and the City*, published two months before, had not brought the life-changing success he'd anticipated; his writing career now promised an ongoing struggle rather than a windfall event.

After an evening at home with his mother, he was preparing to set off for the West and then Mexico, the fourth trip in *On the Road*. Such nights were always fraught, he wrote—"the night before the journey is like the night before death." He had sworn on his father's deathbed always to care for his mother, and now he was leaving. At twenty-eight, he was well past the age of most people who discover his book, and surely past most people's image of Sal and Dean.

"Where am I really going, and what for?" he asked. "Why must I always travel from here to there, as if it mattered where

one is?" He remonstrated with himself first for his latest romantic failure, with Sara Yokley, a former girlfriend of Lucien Carr's,
then began the formal charges and responses—translated, he
wrote, from his native French:

"'You don't know how to work any more, you're an idiot. Arrange your life and shut your mouth. You know damn well you
won't work in Mexico—in Denver you won't have time. You're
spending your money and that's all. Poor dope. . . .'

"'Shall I take this trip?—I have to, it's all arranged.'

"'Yes, go. Go away. Do what you like. Go play, go be the fool.
When you return you'll be older, that's all.'

"'What'll I do when I return?'

"'The same thing you could do now.'

"'What is that?'

"'Work and make your life. Find a woman and marry. Have
children and shut your mouth. Be a man and not a child. . . .
Stop running like a mouse over the surface of the earth. Life's
not long and you're not young.'"

Perhaps the grilling was gentler in French. But in any language it underscores a problem readers have had with Kerouac:
that he had very traditional values, and that he lived a life at odds
with these values. In the sixties, when he repudiated any connection with the counterculture, declaring William F. Buckley
his hero, many thought the booze and bitterness had curdled his
mind. But Kerouac had always been conservative—a blue-collar
son, Catholic, a veteran of the merchant marine and (briefly) the
navy. "I believed in a good home," he wrote in the scroll draft,
"in sane and sound living, in good food, good times, work, faith
and hope. I have always believed in these things. It was with
some amazement that I realized I was one of the few people in

the world who really believed in these things without going around making a dull middleclass philosophy out of it."

He loved America for taking his French-Canadian family in, and so he was quick on the defensive, even as he often felt a stranger or outsider. Though he was never sophisticated in his politics, and few real conservatives would embrace him as one of theirs, he scorned anything he saw as negative or anti-American, including the intellectual Left and antiwar movement. In style, vision and expectations he was a child of the thirties and forties, not the fifties and sixties, a fact hidden by the six-year delay in getting *On the Road* published.

"It's generally construed that Jack underwent some sort of a change and became more conservative," said William Burroughs, who fell out with Kerouac periodically over Jack's loyalty to his reactionary mother. "But he was always conservative. Those ideas never changed. He was always the same. It was sort of a double-think. In one way he was a Buddhist with this expansionistic viewpoint, and on the other hand he always had the most conservative political opinions."

These extended to his attitudes toward family and work ethic. Friends who caroused with him in all permutations of sex and drugs and bebop were universally "disappointed that he had family values and an old-fashioned artistic notion of himself as a novelist with a pipe and an armchair and a fireplace," Allen Ginsberg said. "Everybody expected him to be a rebel and an idiot and angry, and he wasn't that at all. He was a suffering Buddhist who understood a great deal and was able to live with his mother. That's not a rebel."

Kerouac acknowledged this "dual mind" as early as 1943 in a letter to his Lowell friend G. J. Apostolos. Even among Lowell's working-class immigrant kids he'd had two groups of friends, an intellectual crowd and a rowdier set. He was torn, he wrote, between his "normal" and "schizoid" sides. "My schizoid side is the Raskolnikov-Dedalus-George Webber-Duluoz side,* the bent and brooding figure sneering at a world of mediocrities, complacent ignorance, and bigotry exercised by ersatz Ben Franklins; the introverted, scholarly side; the alien side." Its "normal" counterpart was the social Kerouac, "the halfback-whoremaster-alemate-scullion-jitterbug-jazz critic side, the side in me which recommends a broad, rugged America."

By the time of his French self-criticism, the dual nature showed up as a split between the traditional, productive life he said he wanted and the things he did to undermine it. He was similarly divided in his faith, which often seemed more a remote goal for his life than a day-to-day pillar: He believed in *belief*. The dualism was Kerouac's gift as a thinker, enabling him to hold contradictory views at the same time, embracing them emotionally rather than resolving them analytically. As Cassady encouraged him, "you fluctuate, & fluctuate beautifully—fluctuation is your virtue."

The Parable of the Photo Booth

At the start of *On the Road*, Sal's friends see the split and celebrate it—it means he's got something for everybody. At the Thirty-fourth Street Greyhound station, where Sal and Carlo have gone to see Dean off, Sal poses for a vending-booth photo that "made me look like a thirty-year-old Italian who'd kill anybody who said anything against his mother. This picture Carlo and Dean neatly cut down the middle with a razor and saved a

---

*Raskolnikov is the protagonist of Dostoyevsky's *Crime and Punishment*. Stephen Dedalus is the hero of Joyce's *A Portrait of the Artist as a Young Man*. George Webber belongs to Thomas Wolfe's *You Can't Go Home Again* and *The Web and the Rock*. Duluoz is Kerouac's own fictionalized name.

Sins

On the Road is often blamed for America's ongoing goatee problem, but the book is in fact clean-shaven. Kerouac disdained chin spinach, especially on white dudes. "For some reason my name has become associated with bearded beatniks," he wrote his future wife Stella Sampas, in a tone suggesting he'd been accused of listening to Michael Bolton.

Kerouac forgave Gary Snyder's scruff (maybe it was an East Coast/West Coast thing, as in hip-hop), but a goatee in *On the Road* marks its bearer, a sixteen-year-old trombone player, as a sad wannabe. "Nobody looked at him. They finished, packed up, and left for another bar. He wanted to jump, skinny Chicago kid. He slapped on his dark glasses, raised the trombone to his lips alone in the bar, and went 'Baugh!'" Kid might as well have had a scarlet G on his puss.

After *Road*'s success, the goatee myth only calcified. In *Desolation Angels*, in which Jack uses the moniker Duluoz, a party hostess approaches the narrator, "I'm not going to ask you if you're Jack Duluoz because I know he wears a beard."

Kerouac accrued other phantom sins as well. William Burroughs wrote that *On the Road* "sold millions of Levi's and created thousands of espresso bars," though not a single shot is pulled in its pages, and its author, as the ads said, wore khakis. But such are the fruits of defying one's mother, especially one as hellacious as Gabrielle Kerouac. "He never had a beard in his life," she told the *New York Post*'s Al Aronowitz in 1959, "although I think he'd be better off myself if he had one."

half each in their wallets." Presumably Carlo, the sometimes negative intellectual, chose the Raskolnikov half; Dean, the halfback whoremaster.

A novel that begins with a fissure will set to repair it, and this is the lesson in the Parable of the Photo Booth: As much as Sal loves his friends, he must outgrow the two sides they represent to become a whole—to "be a man and not a child." Both roles are incomplete, like the duded-up businessmen in Wild West Cheyenne or the skinny salesman on the controlled starvation diet. Dean himself describes the logical end of the whoremaster alemate path: "You see, man," he tells Sal, "you get older and troubles pile up. Someday you and me'll be coming down an alley together at sundown and looking in the cans to see." Sal is shocked. "You mean we'll end up old bums?" he asks. Down the other path, Carlo appears as a stilted voice of doom, delivering mock-prophecy in his bathrobe: "The days of wrath are yet to come. The balloon won't sustain you much longer."

Like any comedy, the book wants to resolve in stability and marriage, and the stability Sal seeks is highly traditional: "All these years I was looking for the woman I wanted to marry," he tells his friends. "I couldn't meet a girl without saying to myself, What kind of wife would she make? . . . 'I want to marry a girl,' I told them, 'so I can rest my soul with her till we both get old. This can't go on all the time—all this franticness and jumping around. We've got to go someplace, find something.'"

On the Road allowed Kerouac to address this "franticness and jumping around" while still enjoying its pleasures. He could preach maturity on the page without having to live it. His real life in these years was a series of salmonlike leaps toward a settled home, always pushed back by a current in him more powerful than his stated intentions. But still he wanted to make it. Without hearth and home, he felt, writing becomes a "peculiarly un-human" endeavor, waged on "stormy unimaginable seas, alone." He peppered Cassady with plans to buy a ranch together, stock it with three hundred head and "marry a Western girl and have six kids." His new wife, he was sure, would be available for "rushing off to mad bars, yet at the same time a sunny housekeeper."

In part, this was simply the era speaking. Even Allen Ginsberg described for friends what sort of bride and wedding he wanted. But it was also something deep-seated in Kerouac, the side of himself that he valued. He took offense at readers "who 'admire' me for being so 'wild & irresponsible,'" which he considered not just a misreading of his book but "the perversion of our teaching." In effect he blamed them for the same things he held against himself. Kerouac saw *On the Road* as a story of America, and the split in his own character—between his wanderlust and his desire to "work and make your life"—as part of a national chasm that began with the prospectors' gold rush. Their road, he felt, would have its Judgment Day.

The Parable of the Photo Booth, then, reflects the rupture not just in Sal but in the nation. Like Whitman, who is also wrongly considered a rebel, Kerouac saw his work as a healing or unifying force, a moan for man. "The vision of America," he wrote after the success of *On the Road*, "is being destroyed now by the beatnik movement which is not the 'beat generation' I proposed any more but a big move-in from intellectual dissident wrecks of all kinds and now even anti-American, America-haters of all kinds with placards who call themselves 'beatniks.'"

The novel's dual protagonists enable Kerouac to address the fissure in himself and his surround without becoming the thing he disparaged, the scowling critic. He gives Sal the side that wants to mature, allowing Dean to play out the unsettled, impulsive side. By canonizing Dean's pure childishness, Kerouac allows Sal to outgrow his jitterbug side without condemning it; the novel simply shifts the burden of innocence to Dean, then rolls him in it. It outsources Jack's adolescence.

Describing the book to Cassady after the scroll blitz, Kerouac wrote, "Plot, if any, is devoted to your development from young

jailkid of early days to later (present) W. C. Fields saintliness."
In fact Dean's saintliness is more decomposition than development: He becomes holy as he breaks down physically,
intellectually and linguistically. Cars are destroyed, wives abandoned and added, bones broken and badly set. W. C. Fields is a
great character and perhaps even a redemptive one, but we don't
want to be him. His saintly role is to make us feel superior to
our sins.

This sainthood starts to emerge during Sal's third trip to California, when he finds Dean broken and suicidal. Dean has just
shattered his thumb on the forehead of his first wife, Marylou,
and trashed his home life with his second wife, Camille. He
pushed a gun on Marylou and begged her to kill him. (Carolyn
Cassady, the real Camille, thought little of Neal's violence: "He
is known to have hit women," she wrote after his death, "but I'm
sure they asked for it, and that it was a sexual turn-on, as some
have confessed to me.") Now, with a baby at home and another
on the way, Dean is skipping out on Camille to drive cross-
country with Sal, starting with "two days of kicks" in San
Francisco.

But first he is confronted by Galatea Dunkel, the wife of his
Denver travel buddy Ed Dunkel. The scene is a turning point in
both protagonists' development. Galatea has become a tarot
reader—a voice of prophecy. (Later Dean will mock her gift by
telling fortunes with a deck of pornographic cards.) "Dean, why
do you act so foolish?" she begins, humiliating him in front of
the men who were once his disciples. "You have absolutely no
regard for anybody [but] yourself and your damned kicks. All
you think about is what's hanging between your legs and how
much money or fun you can get out of people and then you just
throw them aside."

The indictment is dead on. Yet for Sal, all Dean's trespasses only render him more innocent. As Kerouac told Carroll Brown, God loves Dean because there is so much to forgive him; more sins would only mean more opportunities to forgive. The real Cassady objected to the book because it depicted only the side of him "that he was trying so desperately to change," according to Carolyn. But Kerouac was a novelist, not a biographer, dealing in themes of penance and redemption. In Dean he made these the sum of his identity—his sin and blessedness are of a piece.

Dean becomes saintly only in collapse, losing even his gift of con: "[W]here once Dean would have talked his way out, he now fell silent himself." This is Dean's apotheosis and limitation. Sal sees him finally as the "HOLY GOOF," an American version of Dostoyevsky's innocent Idiot—"ragged and broken and idiotic. . . . He was BEAT—the root, the soul of Beatific," dependent on Sal in a way he has not been up to now. Kerouac's coinage of "Beat" here is his own—meaning beat up and beat down, as he learned it from hustlers like Herbert Huncke, but also blessed and enraptured.

It is up to Sal, who has been a silent observer, finally to speak up. As Dean loses his voice over the course of the novel, Sal, the writer, finds his. "Very well, then," he tells Galatea and the others, "[but] I'll bet you want to know what he does next and that's because he's got the secret that we're all busting to find and it's splitting his head wide open and if he goes mad don't worry, it won't be your fault but the fault of God."

But like the others, Sal no longer wants to emulate Dean. "It was probably the pivotal point of our friendship," Sal says. "Something clicked in both of us. In me it was suddenly concern for a man who was years younger than I." Sal has moved from apprentice to protective elder figure. "[H]e needed me now," Sal says. "Poor, poor Dean—the devil himself had never fallen farther; in idiocy, with infected thumb, surrounded by the battered suitcases of his motherless feverish life across America and back numberless times, an undone bird." He recognizes Dean as no longer a hero in the mythic Gene Autry, Marlboro Man mode, but for Sal this only makes him more heroic. As Kerouac remarked to Ed White, "the modern hero is more like Charles Chaplin."

Forgive Everything

By the time the book came out, construction of the $76 billion Interstate Highway System, begun in 1956, had doomed Kerouac's local roads and their fraternity. Kerouac acknowledged that the world he was writing about was even then vanishing or gone, that his road adventures "may soon be obsolete as America enters its High Civilization period and no one will get sentimental or poetic any more about trains and dew on fences at dawn in Missouri." The Holiday Inn motel chain, which started in 1952, was slowly furnishing the old hobo routes with gift shops and air conditioning and families on vacation.

"You can't do what I did anymore," he said two weeks before his death in 1969. "I tried, in 1960, and I couldn't get a ride. Cars going by, kids eating ice cream, people with hats with long visors driving, and, in the backseat, suits and dresses hanging. No room for a bum with a rucksack." Yet whole tribes of young nomads were voluntarily on the road at this time, in some part because of his book. As he searched for Whitman's America, he preserved his own vanishing frontier as well, a wilderness that for a half century has proved just as elusive and enticing.

By the end of the book, Sal has built a past around Dean,

filled with mythic characters—with ancient hoboes like Dean's father, premodern Indians of Mexico and old prophets who bring the dark Word. In placing Dean in this past, Sal has outgrown him without having to give him up. He knows Dean affectionately as friend, screw-up and myth, but he is not bound to follow any of these. Instead he writes the book. In 1949, when Kerouac was stuck in one of the book's false starts, he discovered this distance and was able to write again. "I decided I am not one of the hipsters," he wrote, "therefore I am free and objective thinking about them and writing their story. Nor am I Red Moultrie, so I can stand back and scan *him*. I am not even Smitty, I'm none of them. I am only describing evidential phenomena for the sake of my own personal salvation in works and the salvation and treasuring of human life according to *my own intentions*. What else can there truly be?" After beginning the draft of the book with the loss of his father, Sal ends it as the patriarch to his characters, independent of them . . . in love with them . . . treasuring them according to his own intentions. Ain't that a man?

After the book came out, Kerouac's former New School professor Elbert Lenrow objected to the last encounter between Sal and Dean, in which Sal abandons Dean to ride to the Ellington concert in the Cadillac driven by a bookie. This is the book's fifth journey and the saddest. Dean, who had made room for the most destitute hitchhikers on their travels, stands pathetic and freezing, denied a place in the warm car. Lenrow took offense to this in a letter to Kerouac. "Since when is a bookie more important than a man in a motheaten coat?" he wrote. Kerouac felt Lenrow was reading *On the Road* as a fifties morality tale—"as tho it was my own MORAL IDEA, as tho I was a spokesman for such ideas, instead of an American Novelist working in the field of Realism."

But in Sal's indefensible act, the book gives readers an opportunity to forgive him, as Sal has grown by forgiving Dean. In the book's chronology, Sal tells the whole story conscious of his own base act and his need for forgiveness. The betrayal was fresh in Kerouac's mind. The Ellington concert was January 21, 1951, and he began the scroll draft around April 2. But the theme was one Kerouac had been developing from the start: As early as 1949, he had God appear to Red Moultrie with the message, "Forgive everything!" Sal's path to fullness, like Whitman's, includes sin and confession. Without it Sal's moan would be a do-good lecture to others, not a blues for all.

By the end, Sal is no longer shy about naming the nature of God, blurting it out as he gazes over New Jersey: "[A]nd tonight the stars'll be out, and don't you know that God is Pooh Bear?" Kerouac owed the line to Cassady's daughter Cathy, and it is the one time in the book that Dean's family aspirations do not appear as failure. Dean is home with Camille, "his most constant, most embittered, and best-knowing wife," and Sal is with his new romance, Laura. In its scroll draft, *On the Road* was Kerouac's way of telling Joan Haverty, the real-life Laura, what really happened with him and Neal. Their marriage, his second, barely lasted the time it took to type the draft, and maybe this is why he later changed Sal's father's death in the opening line to the "miserably weary" split-up of his marriage—the loss was nearer. Sal's hard-earned status as a settled family man is like the rest of *On the Road*, vanishing even as Kerouac recorded it. Growing up, like writing, is not an event but a process.

After his last journey, Kerouac allows Sal to survey the land without feeling the restlessness of Ishmael, nor the pull of his own mad Ahab at the wheel. Ishmael survived by holding on to a floating coffin, Sal by moving in with Laura. Sitting on an old broken-down river pier at sunset, Sal reflects on the people dreaming in the continent's immensity, and on the "three thousand miles over that awful land" that separate him from Dean. The frantic night is now gentle—it "blesses the earth, darkens all rivers, cups the peaks and folds the final shore in." He finds peace with Dean in the "forlorn rags of growing old" that await us all. And this is his moan for man, across generations of sinners and woeful saints. "I think of Dean Moriarty, I even think of Old Dean Moriarty the father we never found, I think of Dean Moriarty."

Paradise Among the Dingledodies

THE PARABLES OF MEN

The Mad Ones

Sal's Guide to Work and Money

The Book of Lost Fathers

[We brought] a return to an older, more personal, but no less rigorous code of ethics, which includes the inviolability of comradeship, the respect for confidences, and an almost mystical regard for courage—all of which are the ethics of the tribe, rather than the community; the code of a small compact group living in an indifferent or a hostile environment, which it seeks not to conquer or change, but only to elude.

—John Clellon Holmes, "The Philosophy of the Beat Generation," 1958

KEROUAC called *On the Road* a search for "the inherent goodness in American man." So what does this Good Man look like?

In the book's most widely quoted line, Sal hoists a banner for the Kerouac nation. Trailing Carlo and Dean as they "danced down the streets like dingledodies," he lets fly: "the only people for me are the mad ones, the ones who are mad to live, mad to talk, mad to be saved, desirous of everything at the same time, the ones who never yawn or say a commonplace thing, but burn, burn, burn like fabulous yellow roman candles exploding like spiders across the stars and in the middle you see the blue centerlight pop and everybody goes 'Awww!' "

The prose is Kerouac at his loosest and most musical, gliding with his dingledodies and mixed metaphors. A man's inherent goodness, apparently, makes him a bad fire risk but a lenient copy editor. Then Sal turns the line on itself: "What did they call such young people in Goethe's Germany?" It's an odd downshift. Why ask about nineteenth-century Germans when your friends

are exploding like spiders? Kerouac added the question sometime after the 1951 scroll draft. Most readers probably just blow
by it; there's a whiff of three-way manlove in the air, and it's no
time to hit the stacks. But for those who take time to parse it,
the question suggests a second read on the celebrated "mad
ones." It refers to a line in Goethe's *Faust: Part Two*, translated
as "Those who yearn for the impossible I love." (Unless it refers
to Goethe's other famous line, *Er kann mich im Arsche lecken*, or
"He can lick my ass," from the play *Götz von Berlichingen*, but we'll
leave that for now.) *Faust*, in turn, should provide a guide to Sal's
adventures to come.

Sal introduces the gang in shorthand, as if we know everybody already. They aren't so much imagined as partially observed;
it's hard to know whether they have lives beyond what Sal sees,
or thoughts beyond what he hears. Dean is "a Western kinsman
of the sun," who "received the world in the raw"; Carlo is a "sorrowful poetic con-man with the dark mind" who does a "monkey
dance in the streets of life"; Remi Boncoeur is a giant Frenchman
who speaks in "jazz American"; and Old Bull Lee (William Burroughs) is "a Kansas minister with exotic, phenomenal fires and
mysteries," whose underlying personalities include "an old
Negro who stood in line, waiting with everyone else, and said,
'Some's bastards, some's ain't, that's the score.'" There's pot, junk,
benny, booze, cars, ghosts, cunnilingus and cheese spread, and
language that moves as fast as the action. "The whole mad swirl
of everything that was to come began then," Sal says; "it would
mix up all my friends and all I had left of my family in a big dust
cloud over the American Night." Rare is the novel that compares
itself to a big dust cloud, especially in the early years of the
Cold War.

Are These Not Men?

Though Holmes got to market first with *Go*, Kerouac's passage is the Beat generation's close-up and mission statement. The "mad ones" were both his subject and his first readers, the ones who reliably believed in his talent. They were not just New Men, he insisted, but a throwback to guys of yore. "Being Beat," he told an audience in 1958, "goes back to my ancestors, to the rebellious, the hungry, the weird, and the mad. To Laurel and Hardy, to Popeye, to Wimpy looking wild-eyed over hamburgers the size of which they make no more."

Sal's tight little crew also provides a glimpse forward—not to the sixties counterculture, which had demographics and money on its side, but to the more furtive and embattled male tribes that followed: to punk rock and hip-hop, and to the men's movement of the nineties. Think about it: With his proclivities for bongos, tears, male love and emotional candor, and his white-guy sense of victimhood, Kerouac could be the softhearted granddaddy of all Iron Johns, and *On the Road* the longest-running men's retreat, complete with mock body paint. (Marylou applies cold cream to Sal and Dean.) All it needs is a sweat lodge. Like punk, the characters emerged from dying cities and scarred neighborhoods, flaunting their pariah status and taste for speed—chemical, musical and vehicular. They chose action and noise over clarity and upward mobility: loud fast rules. And who are Sal and Dean if not two fatherless inner-city males who get profiled by the police, bend the queen's English and largely ignore their baby-mamas (in Dean's case)? What could be more hip-hop?

On the Road remains a primer for male friendship in an age when guys have trouble making friends. The gang's avocations—cars and music—are the things American men talk about when they want to discuss beauty and the sublime. Like Goethe's protagonist, the friends are on a quest for knowledge, undertaken at great risk. As Sal says in Colorado, after the performance of Beethoven's *Fidelio*, "The night was getting more and more frantic. I wished Dean and Carlo were there—then I realized they'd be out of place and unhappy. They were like the man with the dungeon stone and the gloom, rising from the underground, the sordid hipsters of America, a new beat generation that I was slowly joining."

Their road is a male fantasy that goes back to Huck and Tom or Jesus and his disciples, who all chose starvation and travail over clean laundry and the comforts of women. They are merry men of misery, pushing each other to lives none can sustain. Except for Marylou, who is identified from the start as "dumb and capable of doing horrible things," women rarely join them on the road. Even when the boys invite some Chicago hotties for a quick ride, the women are "frightened of our big, scarred, prophetic car." In his one breach of male protocol, Sal asks for directions in Texas, but the other party, a horseback sheriff in a raincoat, is possibly a ghost or a hallucination, and in the next scene Sal is run off the road by drunken field hands who want directions of their own. There are consequences for breaking the manly code of the road.

It should be noted that Sal is not one of the mad ones, who never yawn or say a commonplace thing. Carlo and Dean kid him that "Poor Sal always wants to sleep," and he often gets tongue-tied or says the commonplace. Even at his warmest he keeps a writer's distance, shambling behind "as I've been doing all my life after people who interest me"—a phrase that suggests writerly study as much as love. As a narrator he is a silent fly on the wall, writing the action as if he were reading it; we watch as he does, passively, letting Dean drive. This is *On the Road*'s pact with its readers. We are Sal's travel buddy, allowed into the inner circle, expected to be cool and not ask too many questions.

Yet we are not really mad ones either. However romantic the adventures look on the page, most readers wouldn't want to live like that. The small core of friends who formed the Beat generation was shaped by suicide, depression, psychosis, institutionalization, addiction, alcoholism, jail and early death. Burroughs shot and killed his wife, Joan Vollmer Adams, in a drunken game of William Tell. Lucien Carr stabbed to death a man named David Kammerer who had stalked him across the country. Several of their crowd took their lives: Phil White, who appears as "Jack the hoodlum" in *The Town and the City;* Elise Cowen, briefly Ginsberg's lover; Natalie Jackson, a girlfriend of Cassady's; and probably the poet Lew Welch, whose body was never found—and more went to jail. At one point Kerouac buckled down on the manuscript because "so many of my friends & acquaintances are suddenly in jail, which is not much of a contribution to one's soul."*

At a time when millions of Americans were entering the middle class, Kerouac and his friends paid a price for opting out. As Carolyn Cassady said of her late husband's admirers, "[W]hatever it is that Neal represented for them, like freedom and fearlessness, Neal was fearless but he wasn't free. Neal wanted to die. . . .

---

* In spring 1949, Burroughs was serving time for possessing illegal drugs and guns in New Orleans. Ginsberg was locked up for handling stolen goods in New York. So were Herbert Huncke, a Times Square thief and heroin addict who gave the group the word "Beat," and Vicki Russell, who taught them how to use over-the-counter Benzedrine inhalers. Kerouac had not heard from Cassady and imagined he was in jail as well.

I kept thinking that the imitators never knew and don't know how miserable these men were, they think they were having marvelous times—joy, joy, joy—and they weren't at all." The novel's main draft was literally typed on tragedy, on tracing paper that belonged to Kerouac's friend Bill Cannastra, who six months earlier had been crushed leaning out the window of a moving subway car.

Connections

Edie Parker, Kerouac's first wife, said that Lester Young gave the couple their first taste of marijuana at Minton's Playhouse, the fabled birthplace of bebop. Kerouac subsequently turned on Al Aronowitz, the *New York Post* reporter and Beat chronicler. Aronowitz and Bob Dylan, in turn, introduced the Beatles to herb. And the Beatles . . . well, you know the rest. Kerouac and friends called it tea, Miss Green or Elitch, after Elitch Gardens, a Denver park where they lit up. In *On the Road*, Old Bull Lee appears to have invented a disappearing varietal. Early in the text, Sal refers to Bull and his wife, Jane, growing weed in Texas, but by the time Sal catches up with them in Louisiana, the only Texas crop mentioned is black-eyed peas.

Kerouac wrote his books under the various influences of weed, Benzedrine, morphine and alcohol, which no doubt contributed to the shifts in voice and tone. But in a 1951 letter to Cassady, he ascribed *Road* to strictly legal bean. "Benny, tea, anything I KNOW none as good as coffee for real mental power kicks," he wrote. "You know I dig your pain in any kind of writing. Remember! COFFEE! (try it, please.)"

The Confession of the Alto Man

What holds them together, for the length of *On the Road*, is Sal's search for a voice, one that aspires to the same qualities as their friendship: personal as well as collective, claiming redemption and forgiveness for all. Early in the third journey, Sal and

Dean hear such a voice in a San Francisco jazz club, from a young alto player. "Now, man, that alto man last night had IT," Dean says. He has used this expression before, and now Sal asks what he means. "Ah well," Dean says—"now you're asking me impon-de-rables—ahem! Here's a guy and everybody's there, right? Up to him to put down what's on everybody's mind. He starts the first chorus, then lines up his ideas, people, yeah, yeah, but get it, and then he rises to his fate and has to blow equal to it. All of a sudden somewhere in the middle of the chorus he *gets it*—everybody looks up and knows; they listen; he picks it up and carries. Time stops. He's filling empty space with the substance of our lives, confessions of his bellybottom strain, re-membrance of ideas, rehashes of old blowing." The bellybottom confession doesn't distinguish between saved and unsaved, or between what happened and what should have happened. It just blows, telling everyone's story, not just the soloist's. This is ex-actly what Sal wants to do as a storyteller. He takes in Dean's explanation, then he begins talking in kind. "I never talked so much in all my life," he says.

In December 1950, four months before the scroll draft, Ker-ouac and Cassady began an exchange of intense autobiographical letters that changed the course of the book. "Neal, I hereby re-nounce all fiction," Kerouac wrote; "and say further, dear Neal, this confession is for YOU, and through you to God, and through God back to my life, and wife, whatever and what-all." The let-ters read like trial runs for a new type of literature: confessional and swift, driven by guilt and loss. Confiding his "secret ambi-tion to be a tremendous life-changing prophetic artist," Kerouac told Cassady that he was writing "as though you and I were driv-ing across the old U.S.A. in the night with no mysterious readers, no literary demands, nothing but us telling." His idea of literature, as of friendship, meant sparing nothing, making the private public. In the context of the McCarthy years, when confession had real consequences, this was a gauntlet thrown down.

Kerouac modeled his "true-story novels" on Goethe's massive semificationalized memoir, *Dichtung und Wahrheit* (*Poetry and Truth*), and saw himself following Goethe's prophecy "that the future literature of the West would be confessional in nature." He declared America "the final home of Faust," and described his quasi-gothic childhood novel, *Doctor Sax*, as *Faust: Part Three*. In *On the Road* Goethe returns as a bust in Chad King's house in Denver, like a patron saint watching over the novel.

Kerouac also traced his confessional style to his Catholic youth. Though he left the church in his teens, Catholicism remained a part of his connection to his mother, his French-Canadian roots and the French language. And he held on to the belief that "to withhold any reasonably and decently explainable detail from the Father was a sin."

For Sal and Dean confession is the essence of male friendship: together in a car, cocooned from the outside world, telling all while others sleep. The sedan is their rolling confession booth; the late-night disc jockeys are their jive-talking witnesses— Symphony Sid outside New York, with "all the latest bop," or "the Chicken Jazz'n Gumbo disk-jockey show from New Orleans, all mad jazz records, colored records, with the disk jockey saying, 'Don't worry 'bout *nothing!*'" Though Kerouac described his friends as "solitary Bartlebies," he treated writing and confession as social activities—something shared and suffered by the group, hardened by the company, and atoning for all their sins at once. "After all," he noted, "great art only flourishes in a *school* . . . even if that school is only friendship with poets like Allen, Lucien, Bill, Hunkey & Neal and Holmes."

Which brings us back to Goethe.

The Faust and the Furious

Goethe's story, like Kerouac's, is about a quest for knowledge and revelation. At the start of the *Faust* cycle, the hero is on the verge of suicide because his studies have not brought him complete knowledge of the world. The devil, Mephistopheles, makes him a deal: He'll do anything Faust desires on earth, but if Faust ever becomes so content that he wants to remain in the moment, the devil gets his soul. For a road novel, the bet's message is clear: Keep moving, because satisfaction is hell. In *Part Two*, in which Faust is described as one who yearns for the impossible—one of the "mad ones"—his yearning leads to disaster, including the death of his son, and finally to contentment, which is of course the greatest peril. But just as Mephistopheles is about to sweep him to hell, angels intervene, declaring that Faust's struggles have served a higher purpose. "Whoever strives in ceaseless toil," they sing, "him we may grant redemption."

This too packs a message for anyone who wants to follow Sal on the road. Through Faust's ceaseless toil, he frustrates the devil and is redeemed despite his failures. Sal and his brethren, then, can do the same. At a time when irony and satire permeated the postwar novel—think Salinger, Burroughs, Mailer, Roth, Camus and others—Kerouac shared Goethe's belief in man's essential goodness and redemption. If Goethe's play is any model, Kerouac's road leads ultimately to grace, however wayward the path.

Critics of *On the Road* objected that its characters were indifferent to their fallen conditions, like the motorcycle hoodlums who terrorized fifties cinema. *Time* called the book "a rationale for the fevered young who twitch around the nation's jukeboxes and brawl pointlessly in the midnight streets," and *The Nation* dismissed it as "proof of illness rather than a creation of art, a novel." Kerouac's old Columbia schoolmate Norman Podhoretz denounced Sal's peaceful journeys as a call to "Kill the intellectuals who can talk coherently, kill the people who can sit still for five minutes at a time, kill those incomprehensible characters who are capable of getting seriously involved with a woman, a job, a cause."

The characters' behavior struck reasonable people as irrational, and it was—pointedly so. After the Holocaust and the atomic bomb, Kerouac and his friends distrusted the enthusiasm for rational or scientific thought. They were romantics and gnostics, not shills for science and progress. As Holmes wrote, "The burden of my generation was the knowledge that something rational had caused all this (the feeling that something had gotten dreadfully, dangerously out of hand . . .) and that nothing rational could end it."

Kerouac's characters live with the consequences of their decisions, a fact his critics rarely acknowledged. Amid Sal's salute to the mad ones, he flashes an image of Jane Lee, Bull's wife, "wandering on Times Square in a benzedrine hallucination, with her baby girl in her arms and ending up in Bellevue"—a breakdown of family protections and a nightmare exposure of the innocent. This is the other side of their madness, the dust cloud toward which the friends are heading. To hop into a car with Dean is to accept that these supports have broken down, not just in the book but in all our lives. Even Dean's and Carlo's Roman candles burn only "in the early way they had, which later became so much sadder and perceptive and blank."

Yet their suffering, like Faust's, has meaning. It is like the wild music they love, full of trouble yet somehow healing and enlightening, as the best music always is. As Dean says, "Troubles, you see, is the generalization-word for what God exists in." Their role as friends and pilgrims is to suffer, confess and forgive. Their friendship is not a pact of illicit thrills as much as a hymn to human sorrows. We hurt therefore we are.

Confessing the Blues

Sal makes his confession to Dean on the third journey, after they leave behind the smoldering coals of Camille and Galatea Dunkel. The trip east, in a car driven by a gay man, has been brutal. Dean's thumb is broken and infected in what Sal calls "the symbol of Dean's final development," and he tries to hustle their driver sexually for money. In the scroll draft, Dean mounts the man roughly in front of Sal, "tipping him over legs in the air and all and [giving] him a monstrous huge banging." As published, the man declines Dean's offer. But in either version the driver refuses to part with any money, leaving Dean furious and Sal to digest the scene for readers.

When they stop at a restaurant in Denver to eat and use the facilities, Sal shows off that he can stop his flow at the urinal, setting off a teary argument that is shattering for the characters and confusing for readers. The argument appears to come out of nowhere and to escalate without reason. Dean warns that Sal is getting older now, and to go easy on his kidneys. Sal flips: What do you mean I'm getting old? Dean runs from the restaurant in tears. Hot roast beef sandwiches, one of the book's few decent meals, go uneaten, to the consternation of meat eaters and road epicures everywhere.

Sal breaks. "Everything I had ever secretly held against my brother was coming out: how ugly I was and what filth I was discovering in the depths of my own impure psychologies." He confesses that he doesn't know how to have close relationships with anyone anymore. "Well, now you know me," he tells Dean, who has known him all along. "I don't know what to do with these things. I hold things in my hand like pieces of crap and don't know where to put it down." Finally, as Dean begins to eat, Sal protests his innocence. "It's not my fault!" he says. "Nothing in this lousy world is my fault, don't you see that? I don't want it to be and it can't be and it *won't* be." And they make up and move on.

Kerouac told Ginsberg that the incident was the novel's center, but you'd never know it from its bare-bones treatment. Warren Tallman, in a wonderful 1959 essay on "Kerouac's Sound," noted Kerouac's tendency to become vague or sketchy just when the text calls for him to deliver a meaty climax, as if he were afraid to reduce big sensory experiences to mere words. It wasn't that Kerouac couldn't write a climax, Tallman argued, but that he didn't trust words to convey the music of experience. "When his fictions converge toward meanings something vital in him flinches back. . . . It might become lost, the life. So Kerouac draws back. Which is his limitation." Kerouac's tendency is to tell us that his characters are experiencing heavy visions or thinking deep thoughts, and ask us to take his word that it isn't all huff.

Perhaps so. But in the meantime we have to go by the words that make up the urinal scene. The lessons here are murky, but the scene is important because Sal finally confesses freely. Instead of hanging back, he comes clean to his friend and himself. If the future literature of the West is confessional, as Goethe prophesied, then this is as pure as Sal gets. This is the *it* that he and Dean have been chasing. Such confession is "not as easy as it sounds," Kerouac explained later, "since it hurts to tell and print the truth." As in a Catholic confession, Sal confesses and is absolved—nothing is his fault.

The Friendship of the Lonely

Much of the book's richness comes from the friendship at its center, unstinting in its account of the petty betrayals, disappointments, jealousies and insecurities that pass between even the closest friends. Sal never pretends that friendship is symmetrical or selfless. Dean uses Sal; Sal uses Dean; each man betrays the other: These are the makings of modern male love. Kerouac shies only from examining the ambiguous sexual character of his friendships, a bit of reticence—or perhaps denial—with which his later biographers have made copious speculative hay. His comment to Cassady was that "Posterity will laugh at me if it *thinks* I was queer." But love and hurt he confesses without reservation.

Ellis Amburn, Kerouac's last editor and later his biographer, has proposed that Kerouac was tormented by his attraction to men, and that his alcoholism and other problems stemmed from denying his desires. Kerouac certainly had sex with men and was sometimes the instigator. Ginsberg chided him for not exploring his gay side. But Amburn's focus seems to disregard whole swaths of Kerouac's sexual history and energies, and reduces the complexities of a life and world to a dysfunction that is much drier and less interesting than the books it is meant to explain. The devil, as usual, is in the ambiguities. Surely the mess that was Kerouac's life wasn't *that* tidy.

Kerouac himself sent mixed signals. He often made cruel remarks about what he called a gay, Jewish cabal in the New York publishing industry, and he pushed Seymour Krim, in his introduction to *Desolation Angels*, to describe his sallies as "non-participating acceptance of the homosexuality of his literary pals." To Cassady he declared brotherhood of the sword: "I know cunt is all, I live cunt and always will and always have . . . saying this to assure you I don't renounce the one thing you hold

Was Kerouac an Anti-Semite?

He certainly quacked like one, hurling enough ugly remarks over enough years. He also once burned a cross outside a black neighborhood in Orlando.

But the people who knew him best made the least of his offenses, even though they bore the worst of them. Ginsberg eventually saw them as a form of verbal jujitsu—self-abasement meant to bring humility to his listener. "So this was a seemingly vicious but playful mask," Ginsberg said. "There is a trenchancy in that alcoholic insight that sometimes is useful and in the hands or mouths of someone like Kerouac for me was always a teaching rather than pure insult."

Kerouac advised friends to take a similar view of his reactionary political statements, which by the sixties were equally offensive to the radical youth culture that would have liked to claim him for their own. "Never mind my politics, they're really OSS tactics to bring out others' politics ha ha ha," he wrote to John Clellon Holmes.

But, as Jean Renoir said, everyone has their reasons. It is hard to find the lesson in a burned cross, and bigots often claim the right to dictate what their words mean. It's one more affront they impose upon their targets.

dear but hold it as dear." But in a 1967 interview he described more Clintonian ground rules regarding sex with men: "Blowjobs, yes! Assholes, no!" George Plimpton, who edited the *Paris Review*, deleted the comment.

Carolyn Cassady, who had an open affair with Kerouac while

married to Neal, thought that a key to the friends' relationship was that each made the other aware of his own deficiencies. Both were conventional, Catholic and guilt-ridden, she said. "Jack was even closer than any woman was to Neal. They were soulmates. They both loved each other and they both hated themselves." Certainly the book's comfort with homosexuality is part of its polymorphous appeal—everyone is welcome and anything can happen. But being attracted to Dean is like being attracted to sex itself.

With all of his friends, Kerouac blew hot and cold, especially once they became identified as a circle of writers. In 1952 he decided that the whole circle "disgusts me—The Beat Generation, my relationships with Solomon & Allen & Holmes, Giroux's* repudiation of my dedicatory poem ('This isn't a poetic age'), the brutality of football, the shame of literature, the whole arbitrary mess of my mother's disapproval of the generation and all its modern activities & the generation's arbitrary disapproval of doting mothers, my whole room cluttered with manuscripts, the disgust of quitting just when I'm underway." Like Sal in the urinal scene, he sloshed his disgust for himself on everything he might touch. By the following year, he denounced the bohemian culture in language that would have pleased even his father, as "sleek beasts and middleclass subterraneans."

But here, too, Kerouac fluctuated, lashing out at his friends and then making up, confessing and then absolving himself. It is a tribute to his friends that they remained his friends, and to the transparency of his rants that the people who knew him best paid them the least mind. He kept his worst criticisms, including

---

* Carl Solomon, to whom Ginsberg dedicated *Howl*, accepted and then rejected Kerouac's manuscripts for his uncle's publishing company, Ace paperbacks. Robert Giroux bonded with Kerouac while editing *The Town and the City* but rejected *On the Road*.

his anti-Semitic tirades, out of his novels, perhaps because he didn't consider them substantial enough or truthful enough to belong in his confessions.

The novel ends with the central friendship in distress—Sal thinking distantly of Dean and Old Dean, remembering his own refusal to let Dean ride in the warm Cadillac—but with the sense that they will make up as they have before. All that separates them is "three thousand miles over that awful land," and what's a little suffering between friends? Their one and noble calling has been to move, and they have fulfilled this Faustian bargain; if they were ever content in their friendship, the devil alone knows the consequences.

In the following years, Kerouac and Cassady pulled apart. By the time Neal carried a new generation on the road in 1964 as the bus driver for Ken Kesey and his Merry Pranksters, the two men had little to say to each other. Their meetings were few, fleeting and uncomfortable. Bob Weir of the Grateful Dead, who knew Cassady in the Pranksters, felt that Kerouac captured only "the budding Neal Cassady but never caught him in full bloom. He amounted to a whole lot more than Kerouac was ever around to document." Kerouac had become like his father or Neal's, a relic of a working class that did not fit into the collegiate counterculture.

But the book relates their platonic love affair in its most intense seasons, with all the distortions and quarreling that come with infatuation. Like most lovers, Kerouac is too generous toward Neal and too stingy, protecting him from the things he wishes Neal weren't.

On their last journey together, Sal wonders whether future readers will understand the sacrifices he and Dean made. Kerouac was a child of the Depression and wartime rationing. When he forsook the opportunities that finally became available after the war, he gave up more than the dropouts of the following generation, who knew deprivation mainly as a lifestyle option. How could children raised in plentiful times understand? Examining some photographs of Dean at home, Sal says, "I realized these were all the snapshots which our children would look at someday with wonder, thinking their parents had lived smooth, well-ordered, stabilized-within-the-photo lives and got up in the morning to walk proudly on the sidewalks of life, never dreaming the raggedy madness and riot of our actual lives, or actual night, the hell of it, the senseless nightmare road."

The photos are like the bust of Goethe in Denver, physical reminders that *On the Road* is not a romp on the highway. The circus is not always fun. But for the mad dingledodies, as for readers, there'll be time enough later to confess the damage and lessons learned. Confession is the friendship of the lonely and the literature of the unsaved. Sal's search is for the inherent goodness in American men, a judgment they don't have to earn or confess. It is the destination sign along the highway, telling Sal to keep going. *On the Road* is a letter home from this journey.

And that is how I remember Kerouac—as a writer talking about writers or sitting in a quiet corner with a notebook, writing in longhand. . . . You feel that he was writing all the time; that writing was the only thing he thought about. He never wanted to do anything else.

—William Burroughs, "Remembering Jack Kerouac," 1982

IT is a point seldom acknowledged that *On the Road*, a slacker bible for the last half century, begins with career counseling and a lecture on the Protestant work ethic. In the opening pages, Dean comes to Paterson, New Jersey, to ask Sal to teach him to write. Dean's academic credentials, principally garnered in reform school, precede him. Sal is skeptical at first, but offers his best professional advice. "Hell, man, I know very well you didn't come to me only to want to become a writer," he says, "and after all what do I really know about it except you've got to stick to it with the energy of a benny addict." (The nicer term "workaholic" was not coined until 1971.) A few nights later, Sal has the opportunity to show Dean this work ethic in action. This time Sal is at the typewriter, and Dean tries to lure him off to adventure.

"Come on, man," Dean says, "those girls won't wait, make it fast." But Sal will have none of it. Setting an example for his younger friend, he says, "'Hold on just a minute, I'll be right with you soon as I finish this chapter,' and it was one of the best chapters in the book."

Sal Paradise: writer, traveler . . . *career mentor*?

Why not? As a guide to growing up, the book offers its most radical lessons about work, money and the pursuit of stylish poverty. Though critics had palpitations over the mild depictions of sex, drugs and delinquency, Sal's real transgression is in his work ethic, which is often mistaken for simple slacking. "[T]he *work* of life needs to get done," Kerouac wrote in his journal before the first trip, "and art is work—what work!!" Among manly endeavors, he thought, "there's nothing so manly as the sight of a man writing in great laborious measures and subjecting himself to all the pitfalls of vast mental work."

The Paradise Career Plan boils down to a few time-honored principles: Work hard, live poor, travel light. And when in doubt, let your aunt cover the rent. As Kerouac noted in 1949, just before the publication of *The Town and the City*, "I am prepared for all ascetic necessaries and a downfall of worldly success if so sadly need be. . . . God had never wanted me to worry about bread, first by dint of family aid and the later aid of a widow Mother."

From Sal's first journey west, when he rues his failure in the fields—"What kind of old man was I that couldn't support his own ass, let alone theirs?"—everything we experience in the book is Sal's work, including the voice telling the story. Sal taps a tradition of hardworking American loafing that dates back to Whitman and Thoreau. Even his first hook for leaving home is not mad kicks but a job offer: Remi Boncoeur's promise of a gig on a ship out of San Francisco. "I wrote back and said I'd be satisfied with any old freighter," Sal says, "so long as I could take a few long Pacific trips and come back with enough money to support myself in my aunt's house while I finished my book." The great American Book of Slack, then, begins with Sal chasing one job in order to do another. With fifty dollars in his pocket, saved from his veteran benefits, Sal is gone.

The lessons he picks up constitute a road map to alt success, embraced by generations of readers on the brink of their first jobs. Corporate wannabes and hip-hoppers may swear by Robert Greene's *The 48 Laws of Power* or Sun-tzu's *The Art of War*, but these are basically guides on how to be an asshole. Sal charts a different course.

Like the self-help author that he is, Sal offers his 7 Habits of Highly Beat People:

1. Stay on Schedule (Tip: Don't let jobs get in the way)

When Kerouac began *On the Road* in 1948, he imagined the characters working their way across country at a variety of jobs, including "carnivals, lunchcarts, factories, farms." By the final draft those labors had been mercifully curtailed. Yet work—far more than sex—remains a Homeric hazard along the road, threatening to ensnare the heroes or knock them off their paths.

The danger begins on Sal's first trip out of New Jersey, when he and a fellow hitchhiker named Eddie are stopped by a man in a gallon hat. The man looks ominously like a sheriff and speaks like an oracle. "You boys going to get somewhere, or just going?" he asks. Sal realizes he has reached a moment of professional decision. "We didn't understand his question," he says, "and it was a damned good question."

The man is not a sheriff (or an oracle) but a carnival operator, and he has a job offer. "It's a good opportunity," he says, dangling the bait. For a moment they are tempted. They have little money, no home, no prospects. But they decline, escaping the mock sheriff and the sentence he offered, a future literally going in circles: "the Ferris wheel revolving in the flatlands darkness, and, Godalmighty, the sad music of the merry-go-round and me wanting to get on to my goal." Instead of putting away a few bucks, Sal gives his companion a shirt from his skimpy stash, emerging from the encounter poorer than when he started. This is the code of the road.

If they had taken the job offer, who knows? The Kerouac nation wanted many things from Sal—kicks, Woodstock, maybe visions—but it did not want a job on a wooden-ring concession in a traveling carnival.

2. Avoid Negative Influences, Such as the Authorities

The characters begin the second journey in a state of economic grace, free of financial needs or concerns. But an unfortunate transaction mires them in a Parable of the Fall.

The Parable begins at Christmas of 1948, more than a year after Sal last saw Dean. By now Sal has finished writing his monumental first novel and is visiting his dull relatives in Virginia. In real life, Kerouac never forgave Harcourt Brace editors for cutting *The Town and the City* from 1,183 pages that he felt "ranked with five of the greatest books ever writ in America" to a slightly more liftable tome that was "like 2 or 3 thousand any-other novels lil better than average." He blamed the commercial marketplace for the book's failure. For those keeping track of Sal's work ethic, here's a tally so far: He left on the first journey in July 1947 with half of the manuscript done. By the following Christmas he had banged out the other half, about 200,000 words, more than two *Road*-length novels.

When Dean and the gang arrive unexpectedly from California, the friends are in a state of poverty and grace. Dean can't afford payments on his new Hudson Hornet, and he has left his second wife, Camille, with their three-month-old daughter and no money. Yet they are shielded from economic worries by their own innocence and their indifference to the destruction of cars, which were a sacred fetish of the era. As Kerouac noted in 1943, "[W]e must admit that there is a certain element of virility in ruining cars."

With Dean's blessing, Sal and Marylou make plans to hook up when they get to California. They are children of Eden, sharing women and what little money Sal has—garnered not from toil, but from the beneficence of the GI Bill. "We were all delighted," Sal says, "we all realized we were leaving confusion and nonsense behind and performing our one and noble function of the time, *move*." They have everything they need to get across country and carnal plans for their arrival.

Yet their grace is short-lived. Outside of Washington they are stopped by police and fined twenty-five dollars, leaving them with only fifteen dollars to make it to California. Sal recognizes immediately the consequences of the fine: "It was just like an invitation to steal to take our trip-money away from us." Thus they are banished to a world where men have to claw for money. Haven't we all felt this sadness? They steal food, gas and cigarettes, and at various times consider mugging pedestrians or pimping out Marylou but decide they aren't that type. (That Marylou might object does not enter into their thinking.)

Their crimes, significantly, do not arise from their natures but from circumstances forced on them unjustly, by a police force that "peers out of musty windows and wants to inquire about everything, and can make crimes if the crimes don't exist to its satisfaction." Critics of the time objected that On the Road sanctioned criminal behavior, but on this journey Kerouac carefully places any lawbreaking in a moral context—"a divine theft as far as I'm concerned," he called it in his journals, "Promethean at least." It is the gratuitous police action that creates the artificial need for money, and this artificial need that creates crimes. Even later, when Dean steals cars, he does not do so out of greed but out of a sense of entitlement.

Yet the consequences are the characters' alone. Instead of a romantic hookup in San Francisco, Sal and Marylou end in weary exile, heating a can of pork and beans on an upside-down iron. Taking stock of his work options, Sal feels only the meanness of their fallen world (which for some reason resembles Nathanael West's Hollywood more than San Francisco): "Everybody looked like a broken-down movie extra, a withered starlet; disenchanted stunt-men, midget auto-racers, poignant California characters with their end-of-the-continent sadness, handsome, decadent, Casanova-ish men, puffy-eyed motel blondes, hustlers, pimps, whores, masseurs, bellhops—a lemon lot, and how's a man going to make a living with a gang like that?"

Banished from the garden, they have only lemons and beans, and a management lesson for companies of all sizes: One bad person in authority can ruin things for everybody.

3. Find the Right Career Rhythm— and the Right Office Supplies

Work is a strong dividing line between the two protagonists. Though Dean wants to write—and though Kerouac praised Cassady's writing as better than his own—he comes to life for the first time in Sal's description of him on the job: "The most fantastic parking-lot attendant in the world, he can back a car forty miles an hour into a tight squeeze and stop at the wall, jump out, race among fenders, leap into another car, circle it fifty miles an hour in a narrow space, back swiftly into tight spot; *hump*, snap the car with the emergency so that you see it bounce as he flies out; then clear to the ticket shack, sprinting like a track star, hand a ticket, leap into a newly arrived car before the owner's half out. . . ." This is our first glimpse of Dean *in rhythm*, showing the physical grace that has charmed men and women alike. Yet his work is a parody of *On the Road*'s adventures, as aimless as the carnival merry-go-round: He's driving like mad but he isn't getting anywhere, and his adventures are nada—even the most devoted Deaniac would not read a book called *In the Lot*.

Sal, by contrast, is out of character in the workplace. When he takes a gig as a night watchman in Marin City, California, his ill-fitting uniform hangs like a goofy stage costume, and his gun makes him do things he can't explain: "when a queer approached me in a bar john I took out the gun and said, 'Eh? Eh? What's that you say?' He bolted. I've never understood why I did that." He sends every possible penny home to his aunt, becoming poorer for his labors—a farce on American work and consumer patterns. Finally he turns to crime to support his work habit, stealing from the buildings he is supposed to guard. "I suddenly began to realize that everybody in America is a natural-born thief," he says, deciding that the only way to go straight is to quit his job. "I was getting the bug myself."

Kerouac's attitude toward work, like Sal's, is not always what acolytes have assumed. A dropout from college and the navy, he never held a job for more than a few months; and he ignored his mother's urging to pursue a career in insurance. Yet he produced novel after novel even when nobody wanted them, often working around the clock under physically taxing conditions. His files were meticulous. The son of a printer, he put great stock in words as a material product, dutifully recording in his journal how many he produced in any given day, as if he were laying bricks or clearing acres: "These past few days I've been lost in fantasies and reveries again, the mad & lonely young poet again— which I actually don't welcome, by the way, it's too eerie, unreal, insane, lonesome, joyless and morbid. . . . [W]orked like a dog and only produced 5500 words. This is disgusting." He clung to an antiquated standard that measured a man by how much he produced, not how much he consumed.

Kerouac and Cassady squabbled about work and money. Jack complained that Neal worked too much to buy things he didn't need, "like cars." After a rocky visit with Cassady in California, he wrote to Ginsberg that Neal "is dead," because "he is all hungup on complete all-the-way-down-the-line materialistic money and stealing-groceries anxieties and Nothing Else." Cassady, in turn, criticized Kerouac for refusing to take the many jobs he threw Jack's way. "Immediately, immediately, immediately, immediately," he urged, "not tomorrow, you hear, you lazy lout, but right now, YOU GET A JOB!" He offered jobs, his spare room and even his wife; all Jack had to do was get himself to California.

But by not working, and thus having no money, Kerouac created an excuse to stay home with his mother and his typewriter. Avoiding jobs, paradoxically, enabled Kerouac to work. He needed only a few time-honored office supplies to keep him going, and for these he could turn to his professional associates. As he wrote the Grove Press editor Donald Allen, "All I want is oldfashioned white bennies and a supply also of oldfashioned phenobarbital tablets to offset the benny depression 8 hours after ingestion (after 8 hours of writing) . . . (Also, by the way, I would like to lose some weight.)"

4. Live More, Write More

Throughout *On the Road*, Sal distinguishes between authentic work and the things people do so they can buy more stuff. He rejects upward mobility as a plot to make men do pointless things, turning them into parodies of the American Dream. "They loved to work," Sal says of an Okie family in the California cotton fields. "In the ten years . . . they had progressed from ragged poverty in Simon Legree fields to a kind of smiling respectability in better tents, and that was all."

For Sal, by contrast, in ten years he has progressed from elite prep school to college to a job picking cotton for a dollar-fifty a day, with a sore back, bloody fingers and a homicidal family next door. He's moving down that ladder they call success. "I was a man of the earth," he crows, "precisely as I dreamed I would be, in Paterson." Long before the sixties counterculture, Kerouac rejected the postwar "system of work, produce, consume, work, produce, consume." To Ginsberg he proposed a different formula, no less arduous: "[L]ive more, and write more. So work, write, live, work, write, live."

For Sal as a storyteller, the challenge is to separate his writing from his financial needs. There's nothing like money to get in the way of work. In a funky joint on Chicago's North Clark Street, Sal sees the effects of cash worries on a fellow of the trade—in this case a jazz musician, his usual stand-in for a writer. There are bums at the bar, whores screeching, "[n]oises of hootchy-kootchy" and other trappings of a creative work environment. But as a handsome blond horn player takes the stage in a "sharkskin plaid suit with the long drape and the collar falling back and the tie undone for exact sharpness and casualness"—

the after-hours equivalent of casual Friday attire—the guys sense that something is holding him back. "You see, man," Dean says, "Prez has the technical anxieties of a money-making musician, he's the only one who's well dressed, see him grow worried when he blows a clinker, but the leader, that cool cat, tells him not to worry and just blow and blow—the mere sound and serious exuberance of the music is all *he* cares about. He's an artist."

Sal deflects the Sellout Question in his own work by turning his life into his work, and by living in a way that was unacceptable to most Americans, especially the ones writing checks. A paradox of Sal's story is that he wouldn't be caught dead carrying such hipster accessories as his own book. Decades before David Brooks's bestselling *Bobos in Paradise*, Kerouac declared his hipster role models "fervent and free of Bourgeois-Bohemian Materialism." For them hipness was never a consumer option.

After John Clellon Holmes scored twenty thousand dollars for the paperback rights to *Go* in 1952, Kerouac could have revised *On the Road* to tap the same market, playing up the parties and scenes of urban bohemia. Instead he worked to make the book *less* marketable, undertaking the revisions that ultimately became his experimental novel *Visions of Cody*, which was deemed unpublishable in his lifetime. "I never thought I'd make money writing, either," he wrote in 1960. "[W]hen I wrote these books, I did it as a 'holy duty' and thought my manuscripts would be discovered after I was dead, never dreamed they'd make money." He settled for the rewards of the work itself, which he quantified for his agent, Sterling Lord, shortly before *On the Road* was published: "I've been through every conceivable disgrace now and no rejection or acceptance by publishers can alter that awful final feeling of death—of life-which-is-death."

5. Network for Success

Sal shuns the decade's shining new businessmen in favor of hoboes and hustlers and jazz musicians who seem to come from an earlier time. Twice on their journeys, Sal and Dean descend into primitive poverty, first in an all-night theater on Detroit's skid row, and then in Mexico, where peasants work "the golden world that Jesus came from." In each case, they are rewarded with visions. Instead of chiding America for its failures, Sal and Dean join their ranks, losing themselves in the Detroit crowd: "Beat Negroes who'd come up from Alabama to work in car factories on a rumor; old white bums; young longhaired hipsters who'd reached the end of the road and were drinking wine; whores, ordinary couples, and housewives with nothing to do, nowhere to go, nobody to believe in. If you sifted all Detroit in a wire basket the beater solid core of dregs couldn't be better gathered."

On the Road was published a year after William H. Whyte's best-selling *The Organization Man*, and on the heels of *The Man in the Gray Flannel Suit* (1955), David Riesman's *The Lonely Crowd* (1950) and C. Wright Mills's *White Collar* (1951). The problem in these books, and on many American minds, was the failure of affluence, not poverty. Sal's poor nomads are an invisible fraternity—no longer the hoboes and dust bowl refugees of the Depression, and not yet discussed as the underclass of the Great Society. They are men out of time, without a name. Sal calls them fellahin, or peasants, and aspires to their company.

Kerouac brought no political consciousness to his travels among the poor, nor much curiosity about their lives. Sal doesn't seem to want anything from them, nor does he have anything to offer them. When Kerouac had money, he bought pert suburban homes to live in with his mother, but he also continued to frequent skid row flophouses. Sal is not slumming so much as drifting, unable or disinclined to see the differences between his lot and theirs, sharing their orbit or leaving it indifferently. As much as Kerouac sentimentalized poverty and hardship, he knew both firsthand: He was never playing at being poor.

This fraternity teaches Sal language, manners and courtesies that are disappearing from the road. The white-collar world may have its new cars and faith in progress, but the poor have the obsolete past, an America with which Sal is more comfortable and in which he finds biblical truths. He takes great pleasure in road customs and dialogue, captured in haiku-like snippets: "Them goddam cops can't put no flies on *my* ass!" On Central Avenue, a man baptizes Sal in the ancient rite of guest-friendship. "He went right out and bought a pint of whisky to host me proper," Sal says. "I tried to pay part of it, but he said no. They had two little children. The kids bounced on the bed; it was their play-place. They put their arms around me and looked at me with wonder." He is indeed a thing of wonder, somewhere between the children's world and their father's, on the road from one to the other.

6. Plan Ahead, but Improvise

Between Sal's first trip west, when he plans to work on the ship with Remi, and the last scene, when he plans to stay put, *On the Road* is a book of high hopes and plans that rarely come to fruition. Thank goodness. If he'd gone to sea with Remi, if he'd become a patriarch in Denver, if he'd gone to Mexico without Dean—if he'd done anything as he planned it, the book wouldn't have had the same improvisatory giddyap. Anyone can make plans; *On the Road* is a salute to Plan B or C.

And so it was with Kerouac's life, which continually surprised him when it didn't live up to his unconsidered expectations. Joyce Johnson, who dated him in the late fifties, noted that he always assumed his plans would work out, even when friends could see trouble ahead. He was like the Wet Hitchhiker with his map. "It was as if the power of Jack's imagination always left him defenseless," she recalled in her memoir, *Minor Characters*. "He forgot things anyone else would have remembered."

At the time he wrote *On the Road*, he was filled with such imaginings. In October 1949, he speculated on what his life would be like two years hence. Fracturing tenses to make the future seem settled, he predicted: "[I] shall have had a Guggenheim Fellowship and travelled all Europe; shall have had bought a house, perhaps a car; shall have perhaps married; shall have certainly loved several beautiful women in ragged measures; shall have had made many new friends, and met the greats of the world; shall have had decided on later, greater books, and poems; shall have died further; shall have come nearer yet to God; shall have weathered illnesses and toil, and binges, and lost hair, and gained wrinkles." At 29, he imagined, his life would be settled and homey.

That he never bought a car would prove the least of his unfulfilled predictions.

7. Sell In, Not Out

For all his failings in the postwar job market, Sal was really ahead of his time, commercially speaking. With his louche camaraderie, self-conscious slang and gentle machismo, he anticipated the media economy we live in now, which values men less as productive workers than as sellable images. In the years since publication, American business has turned Sal's lifestyle into a commercial brand, with a name Kerouac thought would never go aboveground—the Beat generation. Since a brand is really a collection of stories and meanings, Sal and Dean did the hard work and provided the value; all they lacked were the products.

Readers who overlook the book's traditionalism and religiosity are not alone. The market ignores them altogether. In the marketplace of images, the novel's "senseless nightmare road" is not something everyone has to travel, but a backstory for the brand, supporting products that range from academic conferences to blue jeans to ad campaigns. The Beat brand recast American rugged individualism for an era in which people tame ideas rather than frontiers. They were the first to conceive themselves *within* the mass culture as something apart from it, a strategy inherited by indie rockers, sneaker cultists and the various alt tribes of the post-Reagan youth culture. Kerouac rejected the bobos as sellouts, but in the end they have done the buying, and Sal is for sale. *On the Road*, intended as a retreat from the new economy of the forties and fifties, becomes a model for success within the economy that followed.

You can't learn these things. You know why? Because you have
to be born with tragic fathers.

—Remark to Ted Berrigan and Adam Saroyan, 1968

SAL and Dean are bound together in part by their
lament for lost fathers. This lament has since spread throughout
American culture, echoing most notably in hip-hop music, the
mythopoetic men's movement and untold hours of beer ads. For
Kerouac it reflected an American rupture that began with the
Gold Rush, but it really came home with the death of his father,
Leo, a year before Sal's first journey. To salve the nation's wound,
Sal has to heal his own, and vice versa. From Sal Paradise to
Tupac Shakur is a shorter trip than might be imagined.

The songwriters of the old spirituals never considered what
it meant to feel like a fatherless child. That was left for the hip-
hop generation—and for their fatherless forebears in *On the Road*.
Decades before the Bronx learned to break-dance, Sal and Dean
took on the question of how to become a man in the absence of
adult male role models. Like the rappers to come, Sal bore a
transparently theatrical name and reinvented his roots using images from pop culture.

As a hip-hop antecedent, Sal may be short on bling, though

at one point he pawns a watch to buy a buck's worth of gas. But he has mad flow and even flirts with a gangsta moment, telling Dean, "We'll come in there like gangsters in this Cadillac!" Kerouac shouted perpetual props to his mother. He was even involved in an early media-amped feud between the East Coast and West Coast. In this case the medium was *Mademoiselle*, which featured Kerouac, Ginsberg and Gregory Corso in a 1957 article about the San Francisco poetry renaissance, to the consternation of poets who actually lived there.

Like that latter beat generation, Sal and Dean were criticized as hoodlums and a bad influence on the youth, but their values were family, transposed onto the social unit of the crew. Their quest was Tupac's: "They say I'm wrong and I'm heartless / But all along I was looking for a father, he was gone." Kerouac would have deplored the menace and materialism in hip-hop, but he would have saluted the verbal gymnastics and mythmaking, and, of course, the hos. And he would have recognized the search for fathers that runs through the culture. The search is his own.

On the Road begins with Sal recovering from the death of his father (at least in the scroll draft) and closes with a salute to Old Dean Moriarty, "the father we never found." In between is a search for lost fathers and for the past that is gone with them. "Here were the three of us," Sal says—"Dean looking for his father, mine dead, Stan [Shephard] fleeing his old one." They have different reasons for hitting the road, but each involves his role as a son. Before them stretch the essential questions of identity: Where do we come from? Who are we now? Who has money for gas? When Sal is most secure, he says, "I saw myself in Middle America, a patriarch." To get there he will have to solve the riddle of his father, and of Dean's. For the fatherless tribes that have followed in his path, the lessons begin here.

The Search

The search for Dean's father is the most straightforward, and means different things for Sal and Dean. For Sal, the old man is a romantic vestige of the hobo past, a mythic grail, like Whitman's America or the natural wilderness Sal witnesses through the Ghost of the Susquehanna. He gives a focus to Sal's preoccupation with the past. "I love this century," Kerouac wrote in his journals; "only, I love the last much more." Sal's interest in Old Dean is nostalgic, so it doesn't require finding him, just believing. What matters is the search itself. "I looked everywhere for the sad and fabled tinsmith of my mind," Sal says in Denver, after a solo hunt. "Either you find someone who looks like your father in places like Montana or you look for a friend's father where he is no more." Old Dean is a piece of mythology, a promise of the past in the present. Finding him would only spoil the game, because then Sal would have to stop looking.

For Dean, too, it would be inconvenient to find the old man. Dean is so vibrantly his own invention, a model for the self-generated hip-hoppers to come, who make up names in the absence of paternal birthrights, and form male crews in lieu of traditional families. Cassady once described himself as "the unnatural son of a few score beaten men," referring to his father's flophouse cronies, who embraced Neal as a reminder of the childhoods they had lost.

Unlike Sal, who is weighed down by his sense of loss, Dean is more autonomous without a father. He knows only what's in front of him; he never judges, because he has no past against which to judge. His past consists of all the things he has overcome. At one point Carlo writes of him as "Oedipus Eddie," suggesting what might happen if he actually found Old Dean and had to limit himself to his father's legacy. Dean mourns for the old man and pledges to find him, yet when they spot a bunch of homeless men around a fire he *almost* slows down but doesn't. Like Sal Dean is better off seeking than finding. "You see, I never know whether my father's there or not," he says. "I never know whether to ask. He might be anywhere." A past is the last thing Dean needs.

The search for Sal's father is more complicated. The book's action—Sal's search for a voice, his desire to settle down, his nostalgia for archetypes past—all takes place against the backdrop of Kerouac's relationship with his late father. Joseph Alcide Léon Kérouack was a robust, opinionated, first-generation immigrant, a horseplayer and gambler. He ran a successful print shop during the Depression, then lost it in 1936 when the Merrimack River flooded Lowell and a creditor called in Leo's debt. Jack also felt the absence of his older brother, Gerard, who died when Jack was four, and who in death became a saint in the eyes of the younger Kerouac.

For Jack, Leo was a paragon of the productive man, an archetype that was losing place to the new managerial class. Like the Lowell mills he'd been obsolete since before the war yet was still powerful as a myth. Leo considered his son's literary ambitions unmanly and immature, and he criticized Jack's friends as misfits who didn't "produce" anything. Kerouac recounted their battles in *Visions of Gerard:* "Arguments that raged later between my father and myself about my refusal to go to work—'I wanta *write*—I'm an *artist*'—'Artist shmartist, ya cant be supported all ya life—.'"

Kerouac aimed to prove his father wrong about writing, to justify himself through his work. When Leo developed cancer of the spleen in 1945, Jack set up his typewriter on the kitchen table in the family's second-floor apartment in Ozone Park, Queens, so he could be there as the cancer ran its painful course. Revisiting those months in *Vanity of Duluoz*, he wrote, "I decided to become a great writer, write a huge novel explaining everything

The Other Missing Father

The father conspicuously absent from *On the Road* is Carlo Marx's. Ginsberg's father, Louis, a poet and teacher, was close to his son, argued with him about poetry and had thoughts about the Beat gang. In 1948, he wrote Allen a two-word letter: "Exorcise Neal."

Louis lived in Paterson, New Jersey, which becomes Sal's adopted home, but he never shows up in Carlo's life. Instead Dean twice describes a Carlo-like alto player as obviously living with his grandmother. Kerouac felt Ginsberg ignored his father and exaggerated his own emotional eccentricities out of sympathy with his mother, Naomi, who spent much of his youth in psychiatric institutions. "[Allen] goes around looking for confirmation of coy loneliness, as we all do," Kerouac told Holmes. "He is justifying his mother by playing madman. His father represents hateful sanity."

to everybody, try to keep my father alive and happy." But his writing could not keep his father alive nor make him happy, and, at the end, Kerouac was typing in the next room as Leo rattled his last shallow breath. Jack was struck by the ink stains on his father's hands. "I feel the guilt of my brother's death and my father's as well," he wrote to Cassady in January 1951; "and only when I die myself will this guilt go away."

On the Road lets Kerouac re-create himself in Leo's America, a blue-collar world of patriarchs and their families, with little incursion from the suburban strivers, organization men and idle intellectuals that Leo would have kept at bay. "The Larchmont commuters are a thing of the past already," Kerouac prophesied.

"It is simplicity and raw strength, rising out of the American *ground*, that will save us. . . . You feel it in the busy streets, especially in the White Rose bars at noon when workingmen are eating ham-on-rye and drinking beer." Sal's notion of a writer was as one of these workingmen, an incarnation of Leo in an age of words and images.

His search for Leo's America begins with a series of missed opportunities for paternal connection until, as his relationship with Dean changes, he starts to recognize the paternal in himself. His missteps offer a lesson in how to choose your fathers wisely.

The Parable of the Missed Fathers

His first missed connection is with a kindly hobo on what Sal calls the greatest ride of his life. It's Sal's first taste of crew as family, carrying him far from his campus doldrums. "I wasn't on the flatboard before the truck roared off," he gasps, beginning the action at full speed; "I lurched, a rider grabbed me, and I sat down. Somebody passed a bottle of rotgut, the bottom of it. I took a big swig in the wild, lyrical, drizzling air of Nebraska. 'Whooee, here we go!' yelled a kid in a baseball cap, and they gunned up the truck to seventy and passed everybody on the road." The truck is driven by two blond farmers from Minnesota, and the passengers are paired up: There are two farm boys looking for harvest work, two city jocks on summer vacation and a thirty-year-old hobo named Mississippi Gene caring for a teenage boy. Sal finds himself matched with an insinuating character named Montana Slim.

Sal has an opportunity for a surrogate father on this ride, but he doesn't see it—typical of his first trip. Mississippi Gene proves his paternal worthiness by tending patiently to his charge, a silent sixteen-year-old runaway of some sort. By contrast, Slim is "sneaky" and "sardonic," a man who doesn't share his cigarettes with his fellow riders.

The flatboard truck is essentially a raft on wheels, and as Tim Hunt has observed, the dark-skinned Gene, who Sal says has "something of the wise and tired old Negro in him," is available to play Jim to Sal's naïve Huck. But Sal is not ready for Mississippi Gene's fatherly guidance. Instead he listens to Montana Slim, who drags him straight into Wild West Week in Cheyenne, where Sal squanders his money buying drinks for Slim and two girls they fail to make. Slim, it turns out, is not a father but a son, and he becomes fully human only when he writes a postcard to his father. "It gave me a different idea of him," Sal says, reading the card; "how tenderly polite he was with his father." Sal can make no comparable gesture to his own father, and his time in Cheyenne confirms Leo's harshest criticisms: He wastes his cash and strikes out with the ladies, and the closest he comes to writing is to mail Slim's card.

Sal misses another opportunity for fatherly connection on his second journey, when Old Bull Lee takes him to a Louisiana bookie joint. "There was one horse called Big Pop that sent me into a temporary trance thinking of my father, who used to play the horses with me," Sal says. He tells Bull about his feeling, but they bet on another horse instead. Big Pop comes in and pays fifty to one. "Damn!" says Bull. "You had a vision, boy, a *vision*. Only damn fools pay no attention to visions. How do you know your father, who was an old horseplayer, just didn't momentarily communicate to you that Big Pop was going to win the race?"

Sal's attempts to connect with his father, then, are no more successful than Dean's. Yet his father is guiding him toward prophecy and visions. Since he is becoming a writer, he needs to be a father to his characters—including, paradoxically, to himself.

Inventing the Self

So what's a young proto-rapper to do? Kerouac belonged to a generation of men whose fathers couldn't support them during the Depression and who as adults bounced between surrogate fathers—first the military; then the universities they flocked to on the GI Bill, which acted *in loco parentis;* and then the paternalistic companies of the postwar economy. Kerouac managed to bail on all three, instead making an identity out of his father's absence, as the hip-hop nation and men's movement did later. Sal's alternative course is something akin to Dean's. He has to shake loose his roots and invent himself.

When Dean ditches Sal at the end of the second journey, echoing Sal's father's departure, Sal faces a turning point. He has been trying to follow Dean, and now he is adrift, lost even to what he thought he knew of himself. His vision of himself as the fish-and-chips woman's reincarnated son, which follows immediately, takes him not just across time but outside the boundaries of identity. He isn't just Sal Paradise, defined by his parents and immediate past. "I realized that I had died and been reborn numberless times but just didn't remember especially because the transitions from life to death and back to life are so ghostly easy," he says.

Amid his search for his and Dean's fathers, the lesson for Sal is that he doesn't have one father or one past but many, an endless supply of stories, and therefore many possibilities for the present. His self contains Whitmanesque multitudes. Unlike William Whyte's organization men, who take on the identity of their employer, he is free to choose his own identity.

This realization leads to . . .

The Lilac Controversy

The book's most controversial passage involves this process of self-invention. In spring 1949, after selling his first novel, Sal decides to move with his aunt to Denver, imagining himself for the first time as a patriarch. Kerouac wrote to Ed White at this time, as if answering his father's criticisms, "I am redeemed in so many ways that I realize now I've been living under a cloud of inferiority complex. But aside from that kind of bull, just think what it means to me and the family. Later, I'll have saved enough to buy a homestead, get married, etc., and I have nothing but books to write. Shit!"

After Dean's abandonment in San Francisco, Sal begins this trip with no plans for seeing his road buddy. His aim is to settle down, not travel, inventing himself anew in Denver. He searches en route for Dean's father, then starts in on his own roots: "At lilac evening I walked with every muscle aching among the lights of 27th and Welton in the Denver colored section, wishing I were a Negro, feeling that the best the white world had offered was not enough ecstasy for me, not enough life, joy, kicks, darkness, music, not enough night."

The passage, which does not appear in the scroll draft, has been roundly criticized as condescending or naïve, especially when Sal wishes he "could exchange worlds with the happy, true-hearted, ecstatic Negroes of America." James Baldwin called it "absolute nonsense, and offensive nonsense at that." A rare defender was Eldridge Cleaver, Baldwin's regular sparring partner, who singled it out as a "remarkable passage" and praised the Beats because they "dared to do in the light of day what America had long been doing in the sneak-thief anonymity of night— consorted on a human level with the blacks." Cleaver saw the passage as part of a "serious, irrevocable declaration of war" in the era's racial struggles, which was surely more than Kerouac intended.

Yet the passage is less about African-Americans than it is about Sal, and it is less about what he wants to become than his desire to leave what he has been dealt at birth. After the lilac night wandering, Kerouac wrote in his journals, "Some people are just made to wish they were other than what they are, only so they may wish and wish and wish. This is my star." His song, like hip-hop, is that of perpetual becoming. *On the Road* can seem without direction because its narrator is not trying to develop an identity but to escape identity—first through Dean and other father surrogates, and finally by detaching himself from all roots. In order to be his own man (albeit one who lives with his aunt), Sal must become his own invention.

In the lilac night scene, he reels with possibilities: "I wished I were a Denver Mexican, or even a poor overworked Jap, anything but what I was so drearily, a 'white man' disillusioned." Then he sees a pickup softball game and wishes he could be part of *its* informal tradition, instead of playing only in organized leagues. All are possible identities he might produce in place of his own. If the book's first journey was about Sal learning to negotiate myth and mystique, and the second about the fall from grace, the third is about Sal giving up his identity in order to invent himself anew.

This moment has been brewing since Sal's first trip west, when he woke up in Des Moines not knowing who he was. "I was far away from home, haunted and tired with travel, in a cheap hotel room I'd never seen . . . [I] really didn't know who I was for about fifteen strange seconds. I wasn't scared; I was just somebody else, some stranger." In the lilac evening scene, he begins to use this dislocation. As Sal wanders the Denver night trying on identities, he wants freedom to move among them—not to be one or another permanently but to invent himself temporarily as any of them. "All my life I'd had white ambitions," he rues; "that was why I'd abandoned a good woman like Terry in the San Joaquin Valley." These ambitions no longer hold him. When he recounts the scene later to Dean, he says, "there was nothing behind me any more, all my bridges were gone and I didn't give a damn about anything at all."

The episode leads him back to Dean, marking a change in their relationship. For the first two journeys he deferred in everything to Dean; now he begins to invent his own history and direction. Identity, like music and prophecy, is a way of organizing time, managing the past in the present. On their remaining journeys, Sal shifts from pupil to elder protector and instigator, no longer looking for a father figure for his travels. From Leo he has learned that being an authentic man means producing. From Dean he has learned that authenticity itself can be produced. Dean's ability to invent himself has been his great freedom, and now that Sal has it, their friendship is no longer the same.

Still problematic, though, are his travels in a more precarious realm: the world of women, love and family.

The True Story of the World Is a French Movie

How Not to Pick Up Girls

The Family Guy

[A]bout immorality, what can I say. The true story of the world is a French movie.

—Letter to Malcolm Cowley, 1955

ON THE ROAD would be remiss as a how-to manual if it did not include some guidance in the ways of sex, love and family. This begins, appropriately, with the art of seduction.

On his first visit to Denver, Sal lays out the fine points of the Paradise Pickup Method. Kerouac in those years was working out his technique, which he likened to his literary style, *raw* rather than *cool*. He told Cassady: "the cool man is a ladiesman, that is, a man usually to be found among the ladies, where he shines; the raw man, is . . . *a lonely fucker* but a more satisfying (physically) fucker in that he knows how to go and go, but can't shine particularly in the drawing-room or perhaps even the boudoir when the lights are still on, who knows?"

In Denver Sal is hoping to get over his failed pickup attempt in Cheyenne, where the Method had left him lonely and broke in the bus terminal. Here things are more promising. Dean, who has been triple-dipping nightly with Marylou, Camille and Carlo, has arranged a local beauty for his pal Sal. "A waitress, Rita Bettencourt," Dean gushes, "fine chick, slightly hung-up on a few sexual difficulties which I've tried to straighten up and I think you can manage, you fine gone daddy you." With Dean's pep talk and prep work, all systems appear to be go.

But when the lights go out with Rita, Sal's technique yields only mutual disappointment and an itch to get away. For a first-person narrator, master of his domain, he has no game. "She was a nice little girl, simple and true, and tremendously frightened of sex," he says afterward. "I told her it was beautiful. I wanted to prove this to her. She let me prove it, but I was too impatient and proved nothing. She sighed in the dark." Gallant that he is, he compensates for his hasty performance by turning the pressure onto Rita. "'What do you want out of life?'" he asks, apparently quoting from his playbook. "I used to ask that all the time of girls.

"'I don't know,' she said. 'Just wait on tables and try to get along.' She yawned. I put my hand over her mouth and told her not to yawn. I tried to tell her how excited I was about life and the things we could do together; saying that, and planning to leave Denver in two days. She turned away wearily. We lay on our backs, looking at the ceiling and wondering what God had wrought when He made life so sad. We made vague plans to meet in Frisco."

Replaying the incident afterward, his libido cycles like his wanderlust: He wants both zipless speed and the slower gentility of the past. "I wanted to go and get Rita again and tell her a lot more things, and really make love to her this time, and calm her fears about men," he says. "Boys and girls in America have such a sad time together; sophistication demands that they submit to sex immediately without proper preliminary talk. Not courting talk—real straight talk about souls, for life is holy and every moment is precious." But instead he makes do with his belittling of Rita and blows out of town the next day, a sad cad on the bus to the next adventure. His poor showing recedes like the miles behind him. "By God," he tells himself, "I gotta come back and see what else will happen!"

Sex

Published the year after Grace Metalious's bed-hopping *Peyton Place*, Kerouac's confessions are Victorian by comparison. For those keeping score—and Kerouac himself kept a list of sexual partners and number of encounters—Sal's trysts include the waitress Rita Bettencourt, the Mexican girl Terry, a sluggish prostitute and a wife-to-be, but his strikeouts fill as many pages. Even Dean is too shy to approach a three-foot-tall Mexican girl at a Denver carnival.

Kerouac's editors de-sexed a scene in which Dean hustles a gay male driver, and somehow Marylou's hand, which had held Sal's cock in the original scroll draft, was empty in the final version. This discretion may have appeased the censors but hurt Kerouac's literary aspirations. While the publishing world rallied to defend Burroughs's *Naked Lunch* and Ginsberg's "Howl" from obscenity charges, *On the Road* inspired no such solidarity. Without legal threat, it was a saucy bestseller, not a cause.

And so we come to the road's other true and noble function: escape from female troubles. Whenever things get sticky Sal can wax spiritual about the road—the search for God and so forth. How can a woman measure up to that? There's no guilt in his encounters, only empty calories and a sense that the world has more to offer, which he conveniently counts against the objects of his fumbling desires.

Sal tries the Method again on a bus outside Detroit, with similar results. The boys at this point are "ragged and dirty as if we had lived off locust," but no matter—he's got his prowl on. "I took up a conversation with a gorgeous country girl wearing a low-cut cotton blouse that displayed the beautiful sun-tan on her breast tops," Sal begins, promisingly. But, as before, the woman turns out to be less a reason to linger than a reminder to keep going. "She was dull. She spoke of evenings in the country making popcorn on the porch. . . . 'And what else do you do for fun?' I tried to bring up boy friends and sex. Her great dark eyes surveyed me with emptiness and a kind of chagrin that reached back generations and generations in her blood from not having done what was crying to be done—whatever it was, and everybody knows what it was."

Finally he tests her with the same question he asked Rita. "'What are we all aching to do?'" he asks. "She didn't know. She yawned. She was sleepy. It was too much. Nobody could tell. Nobody would ever tell. It was all over. She was eighteen and most lovely, and lost." Alas, poor Sal: His friends never yawn or say a commonplace thing, but his effect on women is to make them do just that. The joy of Sal's road is not just that it leads to such women but that it leads away.

While Jesus and his disciples left their women for the road, and Huck lit out for the Territory to escape Aunt Sally, for Sal and Dean the road promises erotic possibilities and quick getaways afterward. And when things go bad, they can always blame the woman. As Sal says after his strikeout in Cheyenne, "I rued the way I had broken up the purity of my entire trip, not saving every dime, and dawdling and not really making time, fooling around with this sullen girl and spending all my money. It made me sick."

As much as they look forward to new hookups on the road, Sal and Dean are happiest when they are about to ditch their women. "I felt like a million dollars," Sal says, on the verge of leaving Terry to return east, conveniently forgetting their plans to go together. "I was adventuring in the crazy American night." And before Dean leaves Camille with a new baby and another on the way, he tells Sal, "I've never felt better and finer and happier with the world and to see little lovely children playing in the sun." Then boom—he's gone. His little lovely children will have to play without him. The guys love the idea of love and the definitiveness of commitment but have no patience for the slow work of relationships. The only woman Kerouac ever took on the road was his mother.

Bodhisattva in Paradise

You might imagine that the Paradise Method made a poor impression on women readers. Yet the early returns, especially, were just the opposite. Joyce Johnson, who was involved with Kerouac when the book came out (she'd seen his photo in *Mademoiselle*), famously described the reaction among women: "'You're only twenty-one,' one of them said to me. 'I'm twenty-nine. I've got to fuck him now.'" Kerouac was single, athletic, uncombed, writing in the slurred voice of an older brother experienced in the ways of love. Any Goethe overtones were lost in transgression.

The reception was not exactly what Kerouac had hoped—nor one he could live up to. "One night I was in bed with 3 girls," he told his friend Philip Whalen a year after the novel came out. "I'm getting too old for this. I try to serve the Bodhisattva's role for them but this ole bodhisattva getting tired." In those years, T. S. Eliot could fill football stadiums, but Kerouac promised more fun on the way home. He was a book nerd's fantasy, a writer as carnal rock star.

Of course it was really Dean who wrote the book of love, and Kerouac—who was shy and passive with women—who reaped the perks, through a process that therapists call "transference" and roadies call mercy. Dean is a walking, breathing hard-on, "for to him sex was the one and only holy and important thing in life, although he had to sweat and curse and make a living and so on. You saw that in the way he stood bobbing his head, always looking down, nodding, like a young boxer to instructions, to make you think he was listening to every word, throwing in a thousand 'Yeses' and 'That's rights.'" Even Dean's cons, then, are sex by other means, equally effective on women and aspiring novelists.

What Dean really wants, Sal says, listening to him rocking and blabbering with Marylou, is a complete infantile experience, a return to the womb. The scroll draft spells out that he is trying to go face first, but the published text is more oblique: "Only a guy who's spent five years in jail can go to such maniacal helpless extremes, beseeching at the portals of the soft source, mad with a completely physical realization of the origins of life-bliss; blindly seeking to return the way he came. . . . Dean had every right to die the sweet deaths of complete love of his Marylou. I didn't want to interfere, I just wanted to follow." Unfortunately for Dean, what he generally gets from these endeavors is another dose of adulthood, in the form of paternity.

Dean's Book of Love

On the Road was published four years after the first issue of *Playboy*, and nine after Alfred Kinsey's *Sexual Behavior in the Human Male*, for which some of Kerouac's friends were interviewed. (Cassady's later character name, Cody Pomeray, suggests Kinsey's assistant Wardell Pomeroy.) To the candor of these earnest guides, Dean added the comic profanity of life itself. He has an appetite instead of an inner life. Sal's other friends "were in the negative, nightmare position of putting down society and giving their tired bookish or political or psychoanalytical reasons, but Dean just raced in society, eager for bread and love; he didn't care one way or the other, 'so long's I can get that lil ole gal with that lil sumpin down there tween her legs, boy,' and 'so long's we can *eat*, son, y'ear me? I'm *hungry*, I'm *starving*, let's *eat right now!*"

We first meet him in mid-romp with Marylou, interrupting the act to answer the door in his shorts. This is an odd bit of fig-leafing on Kerouac's part: In real life Cassady came to the door butt-naked. Where Sal hesitates before getting into the bedroom and sulks afterward, Dean applies to his horizontal tasks the same speed and slapstick energy he showed in the car lot.

As in any comic activity, timing is everything. "The schedule is this," Carlo says: "I came off work a half-hour ago. In that time Dean is balling Marylou at the hotel and gives me time to change and dress. At one sharp he rushes from Marylou to Camille—of course neither one of them knows what's going on—and bangs her once, giving me time to arrive at one-thirty. Then he comes out with me—first he has to beg with Camille, who's already started hating me—and we come here to talk till six in the morning. We usually spend more time than that, but it's getting awfully complicated and he's pressed for time. Then at six he goes back to Marylou—and he's going to spend all day tomorrow running around to get the necessary papers for their divorce. Marylou's all for it, but she insists on banging in the interim. She says she loves him—so does Camille." In the scroll draft, he added "so do I."

But even for Dean, sex is not casual. It is his escape from the rational, like Sal's moan for man—the more heedless the better. "'Everything since the Greeks has been predicted wrong,'" he says. "'You can't make it with geometry and geometrical systems of thinking. It's all *this*!' He wrapped his finger in his fist." Kerouac's equivalent to Dean's manic schedule was his twenty-day exertion on the scroll draft: Imagine Kerouac typing madly, sweating, about Dean running between women, sweating. Both protagonists wanted the same freedom from consciousness—Dean by being out of his head, Sal by being out of his body.

This speed drives the novel. Sal's infatuation with Dean and hasty disengagements from women, Dean's schedule—all push the men faster on the road. The female characters, swiftly drawn and often as swiftly discarded, act on the men like bumpers in a pinball machine, popping up suddenly and speeding the balls on their way. Their role is not to move but to propel the men ever faster. After Sal's affair with Terry, his depictions of women get shorter, until they are no more than blurs on the highway. Kerouac may stop the action to describe rivers, mountains or desert hallucinations, but his women are lucky to get more than a few rushed adjectives. Joyce Johnson, after reading her depiction in *Desolation Angels*—"A Jewess, elegant middleclass sad and looking for something"—did not object so much as wonder, "Where am I in all those funny categories?"

The sex is similarly underdrawn. Though the characters jump in and out of bed often enough, it's hard to say what they do or find there. Kerouac encouraged Cassady to write about sex in minute detail, and took inspiration from Neal's hilariously explicit letters, but *On the Road* is almost free of body parts or tingle. Even the scroll draft, which is slightly more explicit, turns out the lights in a hurry. Sal trumpets the fact of Dean's schedule, but cares less about what happens at any of the stations.

A novel more interested in sex or love might linger in the moment. But Kerouac's interest is in motion. Sal becomes expansive only *after* sex, as when he asks Rita what it is we are all aching to do—a curiosity she doesn't share and can't satisfy. Only the road can teach him that. The solution is to go man go.

In a passage that is often quoted but rarely in full context, Dean looks up from a Chicago street at a sight that might entice other men to put down roots. "'What a weird town,'" he says—"'wow, and that woman in that window up there, just looking down with her big breasts hanging from her nightgown, big wide eyes. Whee. Sal, we gotta go and never stop going till we get there.'

"'Where we going, man?'

"'I don't know but we gotta go.'"

Men have stormed cities for lesser breasts, but for Dean they only make him want to take off. His spark for travel isn't the woman at the end but the one at the beginning. What does it matter where he's going? "Every day the world groaned to turn and we were making our appalling studies of the night," Sal says after they have been in one place too long. "Marylou was black and blue from a fight with Dean about something; his face was scratched. It was time to go."

Sal is silent on Dean's beating of Marylou, which is shocking now but was not in Kerouac's time. Though Kerouac professed himself lamby and nonviolent, he seems to have been comfortable with force at home. In his journals, he wrote lovingly that the spirit of his saintly brother "told me to slap my lady love down and make her *mind*." Yet later, after Cassady was arrested for offering weed to an undercover cop, Kerouac saw it as payback for Neal hitting his daughter. "I once saw him belt his daughter across the room in a chastising crying scene and that's why his Karma devolved that way," Kerouac wrote in *Desolation Angels*—"Tho in two years Cody was about to become a greater man than ever as maybe he realizes all this."

Faster, Pussycat

It's reasonable to read Kerouac's portraits of women as simple misogyny. Women made handy scapegoats for both sin and its inevitable consequence, domestic boredom. Kerouac was never easy with the pleasure principle, vacillating between kick-seeking and a puritan distaste for the body. "The flesh has ceased to mean anything to me," he wrote in 1950, a few months before his marriage to Joan Haverty. "What does it matter whether I gain the meager satisfactions of the penis or not? What has that foul, insuitable, lame worm to do with me?" The experiences Sal seeks in *On the Road* are all out-of-body.

But the book's women aren't really the issue. Men who will run from second-story décolletage will run from anything. The issue is speed. Sal's book of love and Dean's are different approaches to the problem of speed. Sal, whose first romantic decision is to stay home writing when Dean tries to tempt him with action, is always looking for more time. Life is too fast, he says: Boys and girls need time to talk; impatience is the enemy of good loving. Dean, on the other hand, is all momentum. "He's a devil with a car, isn't he?" a Jesuit boy asks Sal—"and according to his story he must be with the women."

Gary Snyder, the West Coast poet who provided the hero for *The Dharma Bums*, likened the speed in *On the Road* to the movement of the American pioneers, recalibrated to the age of the automobile. "Initially you were moving very slowly in a totally wild area," he told Ann Charters. "What you end up doing is going very fast in a densely populated area. Space becomes translated into speed." As the travelers accelerate over the course of the book, the pace begins to divide Sal and Dean. Speed becomes an end in itself. "With frantic Dean," Sal says, "I was rushing through the world without a chance to see it."

The pace quickens on the trip to Mexico, where it finally becomes too much for Sal. The journey begins with Sal for the first time leaving Dean in New York, heading west on his own. When Dean joins him in Denver, crossing the country like a destructive wraith, there is an odd farewell scene before their trip south. As the car pulls out, Sal looks back at his Denver friend Tim Gray receding in the distance "till there was nothing but a growing absence in space, and the space was the eastward view toward Kansas that led all the way back to my home in Atlantis."

If they're going south, why does the rear window face east? And why to Atlantis? In the scroll draft, the view past Kansas led to the narrator's home on Long Island. The change to Atlantis adds another wrinkle. On this trip, the first to go north-south rather than east-west, they are moving not just across space but across time. In leaving Atlantis, they are leaving behind a mythic destroyed civilization for an undeveloped world where, as Sal says later, "when destruction comes to the world of 'history' and the Apocalypse of the Fellahin returns once more as so many times before, people will still stare with the same eyes from the caves of Mexico as well as from the caves of Bali, where it all began and where Adam was suckled and taught to know." Atlantis, Mexico and Bali are separated in space but linked in time.

So begins a new phase in their travels. As Sal says at the Mexican border, "Behind us lay the whole of America and everything Dean and I had previously known about life, and life on the road. . . . [W]e would finally learn ourselves among the Fellahin

Indians of the world, the essential strain of the basic primitive, wailing humanity that stretches in a belt around the equatorial belly of the world."

In reality, though, they are three white guys looking for weed and cheap teenage prostitutes, so foreign that the locals come out to watch them through the brothel windows. The scene is all speed and insane volume, leading finally to a moment of synesthesia, where sound becomes light. By this point, Kerouac was writing with an ecstatic vividness he hadn't reached in earlier chapters, which begs to be read at length. The din of the music

was so tremendous that it shattered Dean and Stan and me for a moment in the realization that we had never dared to play music as loud as we wanted, and this was how loud we wanted. It blew and shuddered directly at us. In a few minutes half that portion of town was at the windows, watching the *Americanos* dance with the gals. They all stood, side by side with the cops, on the dirt sidewalk, leaning in with indifference and casualness. "More Mambo Jambo," "Chattanooga de Mambo," "Mambo Numero Ocho"—all these tremendous numbers resounded and flared in the golden, mysterious afternoon like the sounds you expect to hear on the last day of the world and the Second Coming. The trumpets seemed so loud I thought they could hear them clear out in the desert, where the trumpets had originated anyway. The drums were mad. . . . The piano montunos showered down on us from the speaker. The cries of the leader were like great gasps in the air. The final trumpet choruses that came with drum climaxes on conga and bongo drums, on the great mad Chattanooga record, froze Dean in his tracks for a moment till he shuddered and sweated; then when the trumpets bit the drowsy air with their quivering echoes, like a cavern's or a cave's, his eyes grew large and round as though seeing the devil, and he closed them tight. I myself was shaken like a puppet by it; I heard the trumpets flail the light I had seen and trembled in my boots.

The trumpet image recalls the book of Revelation, where the seventh angel blasts his trumpet to announce that "The kingdom of the world has become the kingdom of our Lord and of his Christ"—a perfect tune for a whorehouse. Dean revs up with the mambo, accelerating headlong toward the end times. Sal, though, is overtaken by the frenzy and noise. Even in a bordello, he hasn't got the moves. Too passive to approach a gloomy sixteen-year-old, he is set upon first by a "fat and uninteresting girl with a puppy dog" that tries to bite him, then by another girl, "better looking but not the best, who clung to my neck like a leech. . . . I was too ashamed to try for the one I really wanted. I let the leech take me off to the back, where, as in a dream, to the din and roar of more loudspeakers inside, we made the bed bounce a half-hour."

When a third prostitute writhes drunkenly in his arms, he has "a longing to take her in the back and undress her and only talk to her—this I told myself." He doesn't do this, of course, but he never quite leaves behind his gloom. The pace is coming between the friends. "In this welter of madness I had an opportunity to see what Dean was up to," Sal says. "He was so out of his mind he didn't know who I was when I peered at his face. 'Yeah, yeah!' is all he said. It seemed it would never end." The encounters with women have sped the book along, moving Sal and Dean across the continent's open spaces, but now that there are so many in the same place, the speed and closeness are too much.

Even Dean's frantic pace is beginning to reveal itself as an illusion of speed, just as his precision in the parking lot was an illusion of travel. He has taken this trip to get a Mexican divorce from Camille, who is pregnant in California, so he can marry his third wife, Inez, who is pregnant in New York. He's nearly back where he started, only in triplicate, with babies and exes on both coasts. "All that again?" Sal asks. Dean's romantic life has become a repetitive loop, losing freshness with each cycle. He is not really on the road; he is simply running in place. With each new family, he needs to work more to earn more to buy more. His charm and appetite, the engines of his travels, prevent him from getting anywhere.

The Big Slowdown

After the whorehouse delirium, the pace moves away from Dean and toward Sal. Sex drains from the story. The spaces open up and the car slows down, crawling at five miles an hour past a group of Indian girls by the roadside. They are untainted by the guys' speed, which is beginning to seem like a virus. "They were a nation in themselves, mountain Indians, shut off from everything else but the Pan-American Highway," Sal says. The girls' "great, brown, innocent eyes looked into ours with such soulful intensity that not one of us had the slightest sexual thought about them."

In contrast to the prostitutes, who made him morose and lonely, the girls have "the eyes of the Virgin Mother when she was a child. We saw in them the tender and forgiving gaze of Jesus. And they stared unflinching into ours." So: *après* whores, virgins. Duh. But more important for the book: *après* trumpets and noise, slowness and visions. "Man, man," Sal yells to Dean, "wake up and see the shepherds, wake up and see the golden world that Jesus came from." The brothel was a screaming caricature of the world they just left, down to the corrupt cops and voyeurism; now they're moving in time to a land before hustle. Without thoughts of sex—getting it or getting away after—the guys lose their need for speed.

Dean offers his watch to one of the girls in exchange for a piece of crystal. He "seemed like the Prophet that had come to them," Sal says. But Dean's prophecy is as dangerous to them as it has been to everyone throughout the book. The watch is the keeper of Dean's manic schedule, and of all the damaging speed that he embodies. As a timepiece it is of no use to the girl, but as a symbol it is the most destructive thing he can offer, a stake in the history from which her society has been spared. "They had come down from the back mountains and higher places to hold forth their hands for something they thought civilization could offer," Sal says, "and they never dreamed the sadness and the poor broken delusion of it. They didn't know that a bomb had come that could crack all our bridges and roads and reduce them to jumbles, and we would be as poor as they someday, and stretching out our hands in the same, same way." Dean's watch is the seed of this world.

Dean has been the book's frontier hero, its cowboy in a fallen world, but he is also that world's purest representative, as American as the postwar automobile: oversexed, mechanized, destructive, with too many debts, too much exhaust and too many clocks to punch. His sexual schedule is like Charlie Chaplin's assembly-line routine in *Modern Times*. Sex and speed have been his angel's wings, and now, without them, he has only this useless watch as a gift. All he can do is return to his wives and woes, abandoning Sal on his sickbed so he can go abandon Inez and (soon) their son. The rake makes no progress. "When I looked up again," Sal says, "bold and noble Dean was standing with his old broken trunk and looking down at me. I didn't know who he was anymore." This is the end of the road.

For Sal, though, it is just the beginning. He has wanted since Denver to slow sex down for holy talk, and now he's got it. His Method is finally ready for its true test: to find a woman and marry.

I wrote [*On the Road*] for my new wife, to tell her what I'd been through. It's directed towards a woman. That's why women like it. It's sexy because it's addressed to a woman. But if I was writing for my mother, I'd leave many things out.

—Remark to Ann Charters, 1966

[I]t was ironic that I acted as his muse and his inspiration when his writing had always been so unimportant, even unreadable, to me.

—Joan Haverty Kerouac, *Nobody's Wife*

ON the book's second journey, Sal and Dean pick up an Okie hitchhiker who tells a story about husbands and wives. Like most members of the road fraternity, he is a gentleman, tipping his hat to Marylou before he got in the car. His story is about a woman who shot her husband, then won his forgiveness and got out of prison—so she shot him again. Two pages later, Sal and Dean learn that their other passenger's aunt is also in prison for shooting her husband. Dean takes it in. He is traveling with his first wife to rejoin his second, arranging to pass wife number one to his pal, and all around him are stories of women shooting their husbands. "Think of it!" he says. "The things that happen; the Okie told us the same likewise story, the trou-bles on all sides, the complications of events—whee, damn!"

The Tales of the Armed Wives are a word to the wise: As Sal says, "Love is a duel." But in its full arc, *On the Road* is a love story, leading Sal from one nurturing woman—his aunt—to the loft of a new love, Laura. Readers who grab the book for the generational rebellion will note that its most effectual characters are two older women, Sal's aunt (his mother in the scroll draft) and the Rawlins family's seventy-five-year-old Aunt Charity, who is described as "continually shuttling from one house to another and making herself generally useful," a skill the younger travelers have not learned. And those who see Kerouac as a Beat

The *On the Road* Diet

Kerouac was known for his intake of alcohol and amphetamines, but *On the Road* reveals another appetite: It has a sweet tooth. Dean's first jones in New York is for the "beautiful big glazed cakes and creampuffs" at Hector's cafeteria in Times Square, and Sal makes his first trip west on apple pie and ice cream. When Sal finally gets off the road, it is under the spell of Laura's hot chocolate. In between, Sal makes nasty sandwiches in two California bus stations, lusts for sustenance in the car of the "controlled starvation" zealot, and in San Francisco, America's best eating town, tucks into a can of pork and beans cooked over an upside-down iron.

Though the road involves a rejection of home cooking, food figures in the book's key scenes, leading Sal to God at the fish-and-chips joint and to confession at the restaurant urinal in Denver. Of the boys' perplexing argument there, who's to say that the steaming, artery-clogging roast beef sandwiches aren't to blame? "[T]he sight of his uneaten food made me sadder than anything in years," Sal says. "[H]e likes to eat so much . . . He's never left his food like this"—until finally, "The holy con-man began to eat." As for Sal, his fate is Mexico and dysentery; some meals are best left untouched.

Odysseus, encountering sirens and unmentionable Greek stuff on his voyages, will note that, like Homer's hero, Sal does it all for the marital bed at the end.

Between his aunt's home and his future mate's, he eats poorly, urinates injudiciously, bitches about his friends and mopes about his love life. His adventures in casual sex consist of: a waitress who yawns and stares at the ceiling (Rita), a "dumb little Mexican wench" (Terry), a figurative "whore" (Marylou), a real whore in Mexico, a Denver sugar mama and "a lonely girl under the marquee of a closed-up show" in Kentucky. Ann Coulter couldn't give a better rationale for traditional family values. All Sal wants is to give up the road for the life his readers dream of leaving. He doesn't flout societal inhibitions; he aspires to them. In a mixed, condescending review of the book, the San Francisco poet Kenneth Rexroth noted, "This novel should demonstrate once and for all that the hipster is the furious square"—which should be a starting point for reading *On the Road*, not a final verdict. So Sal is a doting nephew and an aspiring hubby. Deal with it.

The old-country aunt and new-world Laura bracket the novel, looming over Sal's travails in between. One nurtures him like a child until the other welcomes him as an adult. Commencing with "the weary split-up" of his first marriage and ending with his romance with Laura (in real life, Joan Haverty Kerouac), the book chronicles his years between wives, moving toward the life Sal has been seeking all along, since he told Dean and Marylou of his desire for a wife "so I can rest my soul with her till we both get old."

From Sal's opening words, he and Dean are moving in opposite directions, with Dean newly married and Sal recently divorced. Over the course of the novel, Dean becomes a parody of the good provider, scrambling to support his new families as quickly as he starts them. Sal, too, is a family man, but with his own family values. He uses Dean to get away from his aunt, and then Laura to get out from under Dean's influence. His adventures in between can be seen as preparations for his eventual marriage, maturing him as a potential husband as they have seasoned him as a writer. By the time he writes the book he is *off* the road, settled in a new home.

Though popular wisdom celebrates the guys' flight from family responsibilities, Sal and Dean both have conventional ideas of family; they just have trouble getting there. As Dean tells Sal, in his best W. C. Fields line, "you're ready to hook up with a real great girl if you can only find her and cultivate her and make her mind your soul as I have tried so hard with these damned women of mine. Shit! shit! shit!"—one *shit* for each wife Dean has failed. In real life, Kerouac came no closer to this ideal than Cassady, and managed a lasting female relationship only with his mother, who supported his writing even as she disapproved of the lives he wrote about. But for the course of *On the Road*, he was a believer.

Despite the hazards along Sal's route, including killer wives and bordello pooches, it is a journey from one safe harbor to another. As much as he needs the guys' company to gather his adventures, he can tell their story only by withdrawing to the home provided by his aunt or, finally, his mate. *On the Road* may be a search for the goodness in American man, but from American women it wants bigger, more concrete things: support, cocoa and real estate.

Original Gangsta

The book's O.G., of course, is Sal's aunt. In a novel without fathers, the Woman With No Name broods maternally over the young 'uns, trying unsuccessfully to keep Sal off the road but saving his bacon when he needs her. Before the action even begins, she delivers a prophecy on the state of men and women. "My aunt once said the world would never find peace until men fell at their women's feet and asked for forgiveness," Sal says. If she were in charge, apparently, the book would be called *On the Carpet*. Sal defends Dean against other critics, but he accepts his aunt's judgment as the wisdom of elders. "She knew that Dean had something to be ashamed of," he says, "and me too, by virtue of my being with Dean, and Dean and I accepted this sadly." From the opening pages, when she warns Sal that Dean will get him in trouble, she vies with Dean for influence over her nephew, a competition that is resolved only with Laura's arrival.

Kerouac's mother, the model for Sal's aunt, was the most constant figure in his life, but she barely figures in his writing. Gabrielle Ange L'Evesque Kérouack, who outlived her husband and three children, shared her son's taste for alcohol and was uncompromising in her bigotries, including her resentment of any woman who got close to Jack. They lived together in at least twenty-six homes, usually on the small wages she earned in a shoe factory, but she makes few appearances in his novels, and Kerouac seldom examined their peculiar codependency in his writing. Even his letters and journals describe her blandly as a pious and hardworking woman who rose "at 6 A.M. for a decade while I was allowed (believed in utterly) to stay home write my saxes & sexes." Jack had promised always to take care of his mother, but even after he started making money from his books, it was unclear who was taking care of whom.

"When I go on the road," he said, "I always have a quiet, clean home to come back to and to work in, which probably accounts for the fact that I've published twelve books in the last six years." It was to her that he fled when the scroll draft of *On the Road* met its first rejections. "I am completely fucked," he wrote to Cassady, who wanted him to come to California. "First step, I go south to rest my mind and soul in South and eat sausages & eggs cooked by my Mom and Lucien's psychiatrist be damned (and Allen's, too.)" His friends, in turn, tried unsuccessfully to extricate him from her bullying influence.

Ginsberg, who inspired a trifecta of loathing from Gabrielle—Jewish, gay, radical—came to see her as Kerouac's peasant drinking buddy, the one person who accepted all his faults and showed him all of hers. Their language together shocked even him. On one occasion, when she said in Ginsberg's presence that Hitler should have finished the job, he recalled, "[Jack] said to her, 'You dirty cunt, why did you say that?' And she said, 'You fucking prick, you heard me say that before.' And then began an argument of such violence and filth I had never heard in any household in my life. I was actually shocked."

In a rare confession about his mother, Kerouac once told Ginsberg, whose mother suffered severe mental illness, "My mother is as crazy as your mother was, except I'm not going to throw her to the dogs of eternity like you threw yours." But in the novel, Sal's aunt is a figure of benign wisdom, criticizing Dean as Sal can't. Sage to the young folks, sassy to police and essential to her nephew, she is the character whose story Gabrielle would have liked to read, if she read his books. In fact, he mostly kept them from her because of the sex and drugs.

Like the musicians who fill the book, Sal's aunt is also a storyteller, working without words to create the type of tale Sal wants to tell. When he returns to her after his first journey, eager to tell his story, he finds her working on a "great rag rug woven of all the clothes in my family for years . . . as complex and as rich as the passage of time itself." Kerouac returned to the rag rug in *Desolation Angels*, in a rare paean to the narrator's mother. "In one of her rag rugs," he wrote, "I recognized three decades of tortured life not only by myself but herself, my father, my sister.

She'd have sewn up the grave and used it if possible." Constructed of old family memories, the rug weaves the past into the present, capturing Whitman's America within Sal's own. It crosses chronological time—even new it is old.

Dean, her rival for Sal's attention, rejects her prophecy about the world suffering until men beg women for forgiveness. "[I]t isn't as simple as that," he tells Sal. "Peace will come suddenly, we won't understand when it does." Dean's view of the world reflects his family experience. Cut off from his parents, he is his own invention, and his universe, like his family tree, is discontinuous: Things happen. There are only effects, he says; causes, like parents, are unknowable or irrelevant. Sal's aunt, in turn, scolds Dean for ignoring the ties between parent and child, cause and effect. "You can't go all over the country having babies like that," she says. "Those poor little things'll grow up helpless. You've got to offer them a chance to live."

Over the course of the novel, Sal moves beyond the dichotomy his aunt and Dean present. He believes in mystery and spontaneous revelation, like Dean, but also in parental bonds, like his aunt. He accommodates both views, as he accommodates the two sides of his nature. "The truth of the matter is we don't understand our women," Sal says; "we blame on them and it's all our fault." So he has found a way to embrace both mystery and responsibility.

When Sal returns to New York after Dean's abandonment in Mexico, he is ready to find love and family on his own, beholden to neither his aunt nor his friend. He does not have to wait long. "I was standing in a dark street in Manhattan and called up to the window of a loft where I thought my friends were having a party," he says. "But a pretty girl stuck her head out the window and said, 'Yes? Who is it?'

" 'Sal Paradise,' I said, and heard my name resound in the sad and empty street.

" 'Come on up,' she called. 'I'm making hot chocolate.' So I went up and there she was, the girl with the pure and innocent dear eyes that I had always searched for and for so long. We agreed to love each other madly. In winter we planned to migrate to San Francisco."

The Lady in the Loft

The scroll manuscript is missing the last few feet, so it is unclear what Kerouac originally had in mind after the trip to Mexico. Ginsberg, who read the manuscript in May 1951, wrote to Cassady that it needed an ending. "Write him a serious self prophetic letter fortelling your fourtune in fate, so he can have courage to finish his paean in a proper apotheosis or grinding of brakes. He is afraid to foretell tragedy, or humorable comedy, or gray dawn or rosy sunrise." Cassady felt the book's themes were unworthy of serious noodling and that Kerouac should apply himself to *Doctor Sax*, which he considered a weightier work. He wrote back to Ginsberg, "Tell Jack I become ulcerated old color-blind RR conductor who never writes anything good and dies a painful lingering death from postate gland trouble (cancer from excessive masterbation) at 45. Unless I get sent to San Quentin for rape of teenager and drown after slipping into slimy cesspool that workgang is unclogging."

But the book's ending focuses on Sal's future, not Dean's, and it is shaped by Kerouac's changed domestic status. In November 1950, he dropped by the old West Twenty-first Street loft of his friend Bill Cannastra, thinking there was a party. Since Cannastra's death in the subway accident, the loft had passed to Joan Haverty, a dressmaker with an independent streak and ambitions to write. Ginsberg, who was making one of his periodic bids to go hetero, had made a play for her, but as he told Cassady, he blew it "by being out of self control, overbearing, and impatient with her sentimentalized version of self, not wanting anything but 'friendship' with menfolk, wanting to be alone and keep shrine and have big parties." Besides, he added, he thought she had money but she didn't. None of these qualities deterred Kerouac.

Joan had heard about Kerouac from Cannastra, who told her that Jack was a drunk but a mensch, with very conventional ideas about marriage, and that they should get together. Just months earlier Kerouac had planned to marry Sara Yokley, but their affair had fizzled. Though Joan's lover was in the loft when Kerouac yelled up from the street, she tossed the keys down. Two weeks later, she and Jack were married. "[A]m healthy and living again," he wrote to Cassady, bragging playfully that he might have impregnated her after the wedding night.

This whirlwind romance is missing from the scroll draft and gets only a few sentences in the finished book. In an interim draft, Kerouac had written, "That night I asked her to marry me and she accepted and agreed. Five days later we were married." But he scrapped these sentences in the final version, and when Dean shows up in January, Sal refers to Laura only as "my girl," though in real life Kerouac and Joan Haverty had been married for more than a month.

Nonetheless, the book bears Haverty's imprint. At the time the couple met, Kerouac had been messing with *On the Road* for two years and was still sorting out characters and style. "[S]ince Mexico, I've been trying to find my voice," he wrote to Cassady in October, just before he met Joan. "For a long time it sounded false."

Kerouac showed Joan the confessional letters he exchanged

with Cassady, in part to fill the silences in their marriage. He told Neal, "Poor kid wanted to know why I didn't write my confession to her: so many things would have to be explained, wouldn't they?—things having to do with this country's past 20 years, jazz, the road, sports, jails, the war, places, a thousand things . . . it's better that I'm free not to have to explain too much so can rush in to piths. Incidentally I love her and still have to tell you all about her and how happy I am." After meeting Cassady briefly, she saw in him the spontaneous, magnetic personality that Jack had channeled when he was wooing her, and that had since given way to petulance and brooding. She did, however, refuse Neal's proposal of a three-way.

In her posthumously published memoir, *Nobody's Wife*, which has few kind words for Kerouac or their short marriage, Joan remembered his reaction to her questions about Cassady.

"'Jack,' I asked him again, 'what really happened? What did you and Neal really do?'

"The questions, after a time, seemed to ignite some spark in Jack. He went back to his typewriter, and now he typed with accelerating speed, pounding keys, late into the night. When I got up in the morning, I saw that the clothes he had dropped on the floor were soaked with sweat. And I saw that there were feet and feet of the teletype roll, filled with dense typescript, hanging off the back of the typewriter now." So the book begins with Joan's presence in Jack's life, and the story ends with Laura's presence in Sal's.

The results are a book written with a woman in mind, a confession to a lover in a marriage that was souring around them. He could talk to Joan through his typewriter as he couldn't at the breakfast table. By the time Kerouac finished the scroll draft and a month of revisions, the marriage was over. It lasted less than seven months. Kerouac denied that the baby she was carrying was his.

But, as Laura, she provides the ending that Ginsberg thought was missing from the story, a closure to Sal's years between wives. The "part of my life you could call my life on the road," as Sal calls it in the opening paragraph, begins with Dean's arrival and presumably ends with Sal's walk upstairs to the loft.

The Third Way

When Kerouac finally started earning royalties and could decide how he wanted to live, he asked his sister to scope out land in Florida for a duplex where his mother could cook for him and his cats in one half and his sister and her family could live in the other. Yet even in this plan he had no intention to stay long. The idea was that his sister would keep their mother company whenever he ran off. He always planned on living with "Mémère" and always planned to leave. She was his excuse to get off the road and his reason to hit it again; his freedom from employment and from his friends.

Kerouac never built the house nor started the family he talked so much about. Instead of becoming a patriarch, he spent years dodging Joan Haverty's suits for child support. Jan Kerouac, the daughter he never acknowledged, lived a shorter and more self-destructive life than even her father. "For some reason," she told a contentious 1995 press conference of assembled Kerouac-followers, "I kept being attracted to men who would abuse me." She died of kidney disease the following year at the age of forty-four.

Yet Kerouac never gave up his traditional family values. Locke McCorkle, a Buddhist friend in Mill Valley in the mid-fifties, called Jack "the only person of that whole group who my wife would trust to babysit the children, which probably breaks a lot of reality with a lot of people." Holmes thought Kerouac drank so much not in rejection of conventional values but because he was old-fashioned by nature, and he saw traditional ties breaking down around him. "And yet most of his close friends were alienated, rootless, urban types, and so he lived simultaneously

Cats

Steinbeck had his poodle, Charley. Kerouac preferred the dark side: He was a cat man. By his own admission "a little dotty" about felines, he considered them his "muses" and associated them with his dead brother, Gerard, who believed that "God gives us kittens to teach us how to pity." Kerouac's darkest literary moment, the emotional collapse described in *Big Sur*, followed the death of his cat. "I really don't know how to tell you this but Brace up Honey," his mother wrote him from the far coast. "Little Tyke is *gone.*"

Most of the cats in *On the Road* are *Homo sapiens*, though Old Bull Lee, who in real life once saved Kerouac's cat from hanging, harbors a brood of seven. Jack's cat fetish did not go unnoticed. In its 1959 list of essentials for a "Well-Equipped Beatnik Pad," *Life* magazine listed "cat" at number twenty-one, just ahead of "beat baby." But the dogs had their day. When Kerouac finished the 1951 scroll draft, Lucien Carr's hound, Potchky, chomped the end, leaving the planned finale forever unknown.

in . . . two realities bent on denying one another," Holmes wrote—"and drink temporarily seemed to stabilize his psychic ground." Carolyn Cassady thought Kerouac never started a family because he idealized fatherhood so much and couldn't face the prospect of failing at it.

So what are the lessons here about love and family? Kerouac ends the novel before any of these judgments can fall on him. Sal is in a new home with a new love, independent of both Dean and his aunt. Dean's manic schedule has finally collapsed: Having written to Sal that he would come for him and Laura in six weeks, he arrives five and a half weeks early, so they cannot join him on the road. His trip is for nothing, and all he can do is travel back across the continent to Camille.

Sal has used Dean's road energy to get away from his aunt, and his aunt to get away from the road. Now he has access to both but needs neither. He's found the stable psychic ground that Holmes thought Kerouac sought in drink. He doesn't ask Laura what he asked women on the road—*what are we all looking for?*—because he thinks he has found it. Previous women accelerated the book's pace but left Sal frustrated. Now, in the swiftest romance, he has managed both speed and stability—Dean's world as well as his aunt's. It will not last, of course, but that's a topic for Kerouac to explore in later books. *On the Road* ends with peace and a woman. If you want a happy ending for a family story, it is sometimes best to end it in the middle.

We Don't Go Skating Like the Scott Fitzgeralds

The Tao of Orooni

We Know Time

[T]he only truth is music—the only meaning is without meaning.

—From *Desolation Angels*, 1965

OF all the landscapes crossed in *On the Road*, none holds more of the book's ambitions than the world of jazz. Without jazz, Sal might've stayed home and written Wolfean novels like *The Town and the City*, and Dean might've become a Hollywood extra or a gigolo, complaining that he wanted to direct. Like Kerouac's highways and hoboes, the high-bop jazz in the book was changing even as he wrote about it, threatened generally by the economy and the new suburban culture, and specifically by cool jazz, rock and roll, and poseurs in bohemian black. It was city music at a time when cities were becoming obsolete, a record of the American experiment in its many failures. From Sal's opening trip west, when the empty highways of Bear Mountain teach him the need to improvise, he uses jazz as both a storytelling model and a way of life. A honking sax and a burly beat hold all the ecstasy Sal knows in the world, and all the reason he needs to leave home.

In loud, crowded rooms that conflate sex and prayer, he learns the quintessential American story of identity and time and *IT*. "Now's the Time," Charlie Parker declared in a 1945 song title. "We know time," says Dean Moriarty, enigmatically, until finally he explains what he means: "we know time—how to slow it up and walk and dig and just old-fashioned spade kicks, what other kicks are there? *We* know." Parker and Cassady both met bad, early ends, and both were marked for hipster sainthood. Their story is a jazz story, with a message as biblical as jazz itself: Go moan for man.

Or as Kerouac souped it up later in *Visions of Cody*, his experimental reworking of *On the Road*: "go moan for man; go moan, go groan, go groan alone go roll your bones, alone." Same theme, different variation.

Kerouac uses the jazz scenes to write about writing, or to teach about teaching. He describes his ideals of rhythm, flow and phrasing, and defines the relationship between the writer (or soloist) and the audience. But there are more general lessons here as well. Kerouac was writing as musicians like Parker, Dizzy Gillespie and Thelonious Monk were experimenting with new identities and freedoms, personal and political, reacting to both the big band era and the rising tide of black nationalism. On the bandstand at Minton's Playhouse in Harlem, Monk advised other players, "Make a mistake. Play what you want and let the public pick up." Sal applies this lesson to his travels. Everything good happens to him when he has left expertise and comfort behind—when he is pulling themes apart, like a bop soloist, rather than constructing them.

The jazz scenes also prepare Sal for the revelations to come, teaching him to absorb their meanings intuitively, not analytically. Like Sal's life, the scenes fly in disarray, but their lessons are nonetheless coherent. As Kerouac spelled out to Donald Allen after Allen tried to polish his prose, there was a method in his riffing. "Like Lee Konitz in 1951 I want to blow as deep as I want, for nothing is muddy that runs in time and to laws of time. . . . I see it leading to tremendously interesting literature everywhere with all kinds of confessions never made by man before, leading to a cool future . . . the strange future when it will be realized that everyone is an artist, naturally. And each good or bad according to his openness!"

It's a commonplace that Kerouac's writing has something to

Soundtrack

Never mind the characters: *On the Road* can be read as the liner notes to a jumping imaginary soundtrack, running from Beethoven's gloomy *Fidelio* to Pérez Prado's whorehouse mambo. And in the end, Sal abandons Dean for a Duke Ellington concert. The tracks:

Lionel Hampton, "Central Avenue Breakdown"
Billie Holiday, "Lover Man"
Dexter Gordon and Wardell Gray, "The Hunt"
Slim Gaillard, "Cement Mixer" and "C-Jam Blues"
Freddy Strong, "Close Your Eyes"
Dizzy Gillespie, "Congo Blues"
Willis Jackson, "Gator Tail"
Wynonie Harris, "My Baby's Pudding"
Pérez Prado, "Mambo Jambo," "More Mambo Jambo," "Chattanooga de Mambo" and "Mambo Numero Ocho"

Also in the mix are "Blue Skies" (sung by Sal), "A Fine Romance" (heard on a music box) and "Hallelujah I'm a Bum" (sung by Dean's father).

As for the book's blind Tiresias, the pianist George Shearing, we'll never know what tunes led Sal and Dean to call him Old God Shearing. But we know his divinity was short-lived. As Sal acknowledges, "These were his great 1949 days before he became cool and commercial." What gloom, indeed.

Slim Gaillard, on the other hand, is forever. To Slim, Sal says, "the world was just one big orooni."

do with jazz, but it isn't always clear what this is supposed to mean. As a student at the Horace Mann prep school, he was educated in jazz by his friend Seymour Wyse, and in manhood by the prostitutes at Harlem jazz spots. "I want to be considered a jazz poet blowing a long blues in an afternoon jam session on Sunday," he declared, which says more about his self-image than his writing. In an era that canonized T.S. Eliot and the academic New Criticism, Kerouac identified instead with itinerant jazz musicians, in part because they were cooler. The Beats adopted bebop like their gang colors, distinguishing them from both their peers and their literary precursors. They preferred "playing bop in the dark gloomy afternoon of a room hidden from the sun; we don't go skating like the Scott Fitzgeralds of 'decadent' Twenties." Jazz provided an alternative to both the academy and the lowbrow opportunism of television and pulp—a third way.

Kerouac encouraged readers to make the connection, calling his writing "bop prosody" and comparing his method to "a tenor man drawing a breath and blowing a phrase on his saxophone, till he runs out of breath, and when he does, his sentence, his statement's been made. . . . That's how I therefore separate my sentences, as breath separations of the mind. . . . Then there's the raciness and freedom and humor of jazz instead of all that dreary analysis." He used dashes as a musician would, to leap forward into the next idea, not to modify the previous. When editors tried to change the dashes, he defended them in musical terms, as visible cues to readers to jump with the beat. Everything, he argued, is *definitely released by the dash.*

But as a label, his connection to jazz explains little about him or *On the Road.* You can't sing the book or swing it. How, exactly, is his writing like jazz? Kerouac himself was fickle in claiming his jazzness, especially once rock started to steal its shine. He was never a rocker, and when he tried to go denim in '53, his girl-friend, Alene Lee, the heroine of *The Subterraneans*, told him he looked silly. Yet he toyed with changing his book title to *Rock and Roll Road* in order to "double the sales," and he told Carolyn Cassady that "it's the original daddy of rock'n roll books."

What *It* Is

The best way into the jazz scenes in *On the Road* is the way Kerouac throws us there, headfirst. After all the travel and open spaces, Sal compresses the sensations of the road into rundown bars where there's barely room to move. These clubs are off the safe and narrow, as forbidding as the road itself, but they are the place to be. Instead of describing the music, Sal leaps into it, sprinting to keep up, until all he can do is sputter into pure sound:

Out we jumped in the warm, mad night, hearing a wild tenorman bawling horn across the way, going "EE-YAH! EE-YAH! EE-YAH!" and hands clapping to the beat and folks yelling, "Go, go, go!" Dean was already racing across the street with his thumb in the air, yelling, "Blow, man, blow!" A bunch of colored men in Saturday-night suits were whooping it up in front. It was a sawdust saloon with a small bandstand on which the fellows huddled with their hats on, blowing over people's heads, a crazy place; crazy floppy women wandered around sometimes in their bathrobes, bottles clanked in alleys. In back of the joint in a dark corridor beyond the splattered toilets scores of men and women stood against the wall drinking wine-spodiodi and spitting at the stars—wine and whiskey. The behatted tenorman was blowing at the peak of a wonderfully satisfactory free idea, a rising and falling riff that went from "EE-yah!" to a crazier "EE-de-lee-yah!" and blasted along to the rolling crash of butt-scarred drums hammered by a big brutal Negro with a bullneck who didn't give a damn about anything but punishing his busted tubs, crash, rattle-ti-boom, crash. Uproars of music and the tenorman *had it* and everybody knew he had it.

Check the way he explains wine-spodiodi, arriving a beat late because the action is moving so fast.

Though a few well-known musicians wander into *On the Road*, most of the players are nameless journeymen who just want to call down the spirit. The gigs are oases of integration, both on the bandstand and in the crowd. The soloists don't speak their own minds, but everyone's. Drummers tumble their beats down staircases and trumpets flare magnificently, and a tenor man "decided to blow his top and crouched down and held a high C for a long time as everything else crashed along and the cries increased," until finally there were "no more phrases, just cries, cries, 'Baugh' and down to 'Beep!' and up to *'EEEEE!'*" You can imagine Sal and Dean crossing the awful continent for a sniff of the blind pianist George Shearing's empty chair or an earful of Slim Gaillard's righteous jive talk, in which everything is orooni. And you would be there with them if you could, with the other saints and misfits—nodding, as Kerouac later proposed, with the affirmative vision of the music, a generation "nodding in the smoky dimness, nodding to the music, 'Yes, yes, yes.'"

Kerouac doesn't distinguish the music from the experience of hearing it. He is all verbs and metaphors, pushing readers inside the moment rather than describing it omnisciently from the outside. There are no flatted fifths or walking bass lines, but women in bathrobes and "innumerable choruses with amazing chords that mounted higher and higher till the sweat splashed all over the piano and everybody listened in awe and fright." He draws the music the way he does his characters, incompletely, not because he's using it as a stand-in for a sociological phenomenon, as many writers of the time did—say, the sound of the African-American working class—but because Sal sees only what he sees. He deals in observation and experience, not synthesis. His moments exceed his comprehension; like his enthusiasms, which always seem born yesterday, the jazz ecstasies deny all context or proportion. Why else would anyone choose the battered, track-marked lives these men led, except for the moment of grace that obliterated all other consciousness?

In the jazz scenes, ideas come into being physically rather than intellectually, and everybody in the room understands them without needing to speak them. The musicians tell their story the way Sal wants to tell his, converting experience directly to art without analytical processes (in Sal's eyes, at least). Their lives mingle with their audiences', no difference, and you can't tell whether the thoughts on the page belong to Sal or the person he's writing about, "because here we were dealing with the pit and prune-juice of poor beat life itself in the god-awful streets of man." The revelations are visceral, beyond reason, "all great moments of laughter and understanding for [the alto man] and everyone else who heard." In contrast to the outside world, people in the club are most dignified when most out of their heads. Ecstasy is all.

Sal's Paradise

In these after-hours classrooms, music takes the place of space, and rhythm does the work of travel. On the verge of his first steps west, Sal muses, "as I sat there listening to that sound of the night which bop has come to represent for all of us, I thought of all my friends from one end of the country to the other and how they were really all in the same vast backyard doing something so frantic and rushing-about." The music crosses continents, unifying believers in its big twitchy beat. Bop is the night converted into sound, falling at the same time over everyone. All you have to do is dig. Later Dean makes a similar observation about the natural elements, seeing "all things tied together all over like rain connecting everybody the world over by chain touch." Rain and bebop—both communicate God to everyone at once, without word or individuation.

Kerouac merged the jazz passages from *Road* and *Visions of Cody* into an essay called "Jazz of the Beat Generation," which he published in 1955 under the name Jean-Louis. (He was dodging Joan Haverty at the time.) In it he expanded on the connection between jazz and the elements, and used Lester Young in an extended metaphor about us all—about our heritage and the stories we tell about ourselves. The passage barely mentions music, but Kerouac's meaning is all jazz. Lester, he writes, "is the greatness of America in a single Negro musician—he is just like the river, the river starts in near Butte, Montana, in frozen snow caps (Three Forks) and meanders on down across states and entire territorial areas of dun bleak land with hawthorn crackling in the sleet, picks up rivers at Bismarck, Omaha, and St. Louis just north, another at Kay-ro, another in Arkansas, Tennessee, comes deluging on New Orleans with muddy news from the land and a roar of subterranean excitement that is like the vibration of the entire land sucked of its gut in mad midnight, fevered, hot . . . and a gal sprawled in it legs spread in brown cotton stockings, bleeding at belted mouth, moaning 'yes' as Lester, horn placed, has started blowing, 'blow for me mother blow for me.'" This is how stories become life in America, in tidal forces like the river, sweeping up everything they meet along the way and ending with a moan. Lester speaks the city and the wilderness in a single stroke, knowing and untamed, hip and timeless.

Kerouac likened himself in his journals to Tolstoy, and there's an echo here of the famous first line of *Anna Karenina*, about how happy families are all alike, etc. The line is often read to mean that unhappy families make better copy, but the point is the opposite: that there is only one happiness, dissolving all individual selves within it. This is a story that Sal is trying to tell, about the misery that his friends feel individually and the ecstasy that is the same for all, because it subsumes their differences. Since there are as many forms of unhappiness as there are selves, to be happy in Tolstoy's sense, or Sal's, you must subordinate your self to something bigger.

In Kerouac's jazz scenes, the leveling force is the music, which merges everyone in its sweep. It's all pit and prune-juice of poor beat life. The alto player, Sal says, fills "empty space with the substance of our lives," and "everybody knows it's not the tune that counts but IT." This is the out-of-body experience that Sal seeks. He tastes it as a form of misery in the lilac evening scene, when he lets go of his identity and the ambitions that have come with it. The gentler side opens to him in jazz, which dissolves complete strangers in the same wail and rhythm; their aspirations are only to remain that way forever. Finally Sal gives up the boundaries of self entirely in Mexico, when he prostrates himself on the cool steel roof of the car, commingling his blood with the insects that feed on him. "For the first time in my life the weather was not something that touched me, that caressed me, froze or sweated me, but became me," he says. "The atmosphere and I became the same." The jazz scenes have helped him get here.

I've used the word "jazz" as if it signified a static, monolithic entity. Of course it doesn't, and it certainly didn't for Kerouac, who was a jazz critic back at Horace Mann and interviewed Count Basie for the school paper. In Sal's years, jazz was a living argument. The musicians who surfaced in Kerouac's New York after the war were making music that was deliberately hard to play and alienating for some listeners. Cab Calloway famously called bebop "Chinese music," and Louis Armstrong complained, "You got no melody to remember and no beat to dance to." The bop musicians simply turned their backs. Like the Beats, they were a tribe of self-selected exiles, part urban, part nomadic.

To listen to bop in those years, Holmes said, was to take sides, to declare membership in a fraternity of undesirables. "[Y]ou were acknowledging that you had become a different sort of person than the Swing or Dixie fan you had been, because, with Bird, you had to *dig* to know; you had to be able to intuit on the bias, to hear music *being* music, to comprehend the difference between the confining intelligence and the soul directly recording its own drift. No one who was not involved in the Bop revolt can know all that it meant to us. If a person dug Bop, we knew something about his sex life, his kick in literature and the arts, his attitudes toward joy, violence, Negroes and the very processes of awareness."

Dressed in the goatees and berets of French existentialists, the musicians were studious without being bookish, complex without losing the physical. Kerouac likened them to twelfth-century monks, admiring their work ethic and professionalism even outside the economy's gears: "On cold corners they stood three backs to one another, facing all the winds, bent—lips don't care—miserable cold and broke—waiting like witchdoctors—saying, 'Everything belongs to me because I am poor.'" This could be Sal's story as well as Bird's or Monk's. They were outsiders by choice, driven further outside by the unfairness of the world. This reasonated with Kerouac. He wrote to Malcolm Cowley, "every single original musical genius in America, for instance, has been in jail or prison; I assure you the same holds true for literature; this is the time."

The History of EE-YAH

On the Road treats the music as a historical arc, played out alongside the nation's. The book takes place at a moment of change in both histories. "At this time, 1947," Sal observes, "the fellows in the Loop blew, but with a tired air, because bop was somewhere between its Charlie Parker Ornithology period and another period that began with Miles Davis." Parker in 1946 had disappeared briefly into Camarillo State Hospital in California for rehab of his nerves and junk-wearied body. The new period on the horizon was cool jazz, ushered in with Miles's "Birth of the Cool" sides, recorded with Gil Evans in 1949 and 1950. Though cool or West Coast jazz became a swank soundtrack for collegiate swingers and bohemians—the folks who read Kerouac's books—Sal clings instead to the wilder sounds that came before. He sees the advent of cool like the arrival of the postwar middle class, steadily pushing out the cowboys and hoboes and bluesmen and prophets that he loves.

Sal and Dean are on the losing side of this arc. Playing basketball against two younger kids, they fall to the kids' easy cool. "We were like hotrock blackbelly tenorman *Mad* of American back-alley go-music trying to play basketball against Stan Getz and Cool Charlie. They thought we were crazy." The kids simply grab the ball from them and score without sweat. Even among hipsters, Kerouac said, tribal divisions were being drawn between "the Cool, bearded, sitting without moving in cafes, with their unfriendly girls dressed in black, who say nothing; and the Hot, crazy, talkative, mad shining eyes, running from bar to bar only to be ignored by the cool subterraneans. I guess I'm still with the hot ones. When I walk into a club playing jazz, I still want to shout: 'Blow, Man, Blow.'" As consolation, though, the cool hipsters "cooled it in dead silence before formal and excellent musical groups like Lennie Tristano or Miles Davis."

For Sal, cool jazz was not just a sound but a symptom—coldly efficient on the basketball court or in the suburban development, but lacking the savor of the game. "What we Beats are against is technique and efficiency," Kerouac told an interviewer, equating cool with commerce and consumption. "Everyone in this country is a slave to the Deepfreeze and the hi-fi. They're too rich—a kind of sinister luxury." This sense of decline permeates the music in *On the Road*. Even after a heaving, sweating, revelatory performance by Old God Shearing, Sal cannot help but lament, "these were his great 1949 days before he became cool and commercial," a slap for which there is no rejoinder. The old gods are not what they once were. Jazz becomes a shorthand for both America's genius and its lost heights.

Orooni! How to Get It, How to Use It

But Sal is a storyteller, and mainly what he needs from jazz is a way to tell a story. This is Sal's prophetic mission—to learn a style or voice, and to lead his life according to its narrative parameters. If he were a plumber or a lover, jazz might teach him to unclog a pipe or elicit a sigh. Writing to Cassady in 1949, while he was still searching for this voice, Kerouac teased, "Let's you and I revolutionize American letters and drink Champagne with Hollywood starlets. How much you want to bet I can lead us to this?"

In *On the Road*, Kerouac describes one mode of storytelling in the rag rug that Sal's aunt weaves, which twines the shards of the past into the present. But Sal doesn't have the patience for that kind of storytelling. Instead he has the bursts of energy and volatility that he hears in music: in Dexter Gordon and Wardell Gray "blowing their tops before a screaming audience that gave the record fantastic frenzied volume," or Billie Holiday singing "Lover Man" so that the words lose their meaning, and all you hear is "a woman stroking her man's hair in soft lamplight." The blowing by Gordon and Gray saves Sal from his Southern relatives' dull whining "about the weather, the crops, and the general weary recapitulation of who had a baby, who got a new house, and so on"—the ways in which unhappy families are all uniquely unhappy. The music is purposeful and disruptive, beginning at full tilt and staying there. But this disruption, Sal realizes, doesn't turn off. Listening to Dean crank the record, Sal sees that "The madness of Dean had bloomed into a weird flower."

As a model for Sal's storytelling, the music provides a release from words and rational argument, into a voice he considers more universal. "[T]he only truth is music," Kerouac wrote— "the only meaning is without meaning—Music blends with the heartbeat universe and we forget the brain beat." If he could, he would've written pure sound, trusting readers to comprehend the divine between the lines. "IT'S NOT THE WORDS THAT

COUNT," he noted in his journal, "BUT THE RUSH OF TRUTH WHICH USES WORDS FOR ITS PURPOSES." He once complained to Holmes that his young readers were unwilling to follow him into this nonrational realm. "These kids are really interested in you," he wrote. "And the reason is, they WANT analytical prose passages, they want certain things explained, which I dont satisfy in my narrative eagerness." The music, however complex formally, communicates without such explanation.

Sal loves Dean's gibberish for just this reason. Though words fail Dean, his music hits Sal with the rush of truth. Gordon Lish, who met Cassady during his Merry Prankster years, called him "without doubt one of the greatest minds I've ever known—certainly the quickest intelligence. And I've known Nobel Prize winners." You might not know it from *On the Road*. Dean enters spewing nonsense, and in his descent into W. C. Fields sainthood becomes progressively more incoherent, until he is practically singing scat syllables.

> "Ah—ah—you must listen to hear." We listened, all ears. But he forgot what he wanted to say. "Really listen—ahem. Look, dear Sal—sweet Laura—I've come—I'm gone—but wait—ah yes." And he stared with rocky sorrow into his hands. "Can't talk no more—do you understand that it is—or might be—But listen!" We all listened. He was listening to sounds in the night. "Yes!" he whispered with awe. "But you see—no need to talk any more—and further."
>
> "But why did you come so soon, Dean?"
>
> "Ah," he said, looking at me as if for the first time, "so soon, yes. We—we'll know—that is, I don't know. I came on the railroad pass—cabooses—old hard-bench coaches—

Texas—played flute and wooden sweet potato all the way."
He took out his new wooden flute. He played a few squeaky
notes on it and jumped up and down in his stocking feet.
"See?" he said. "But of course, Sal, I can talk as soon as ever
and have many things to say to you in fact with my own
little bangtail mind I've been reading and reading this gone
Proust all the way across the country and digging a great
number of things I'll never have TIME to tell you about and
we STILL haven't talked of Mexico and our parting there in
fever—but no need to talk. Absolutely, now, yes?"

Yet all this speaks volumes to Sal, for whom "Dean's intelligence was every bit as formal and shining and complete" as that
of his other friends, but "without the tedious intellectualness."
For Sal it's enough that Dean *mentions* Proust; he doesn't need
to spell out what he found. Sal notes "a kind of holy lightning I
saw flashing from his excitement and his visions, which he described so torrentially that people in buses looked around to see
the 'overexcited nut.'"

Dean's talk is like his driving: hyperfast, intuitive, combining
words or swerves in virtuosic rhythm, but for ends that defy
common sense. Since they're not going anywhere, why steal cars
to get there, or drive them at 110 miles per? And since "in those
days he really didn't know what he was talking about," why rap
so prolixly? Critics read Dean as a subliterate psychopath, but
he is inarticulate only if you insist that coherence lies in the
meanings of words and not the spell created by their delivery or
rhythm.

This is not how Sal hears it. He recognizes Dean's turbulence
as musical. Dean might scare commuters on a bus, but in a jazz
club everyone gets it. As Dean sweats over a tenor player, "the

man noticed and laughed in his horn a long quivering crazy laugh, and everybody else laughed and they rocked and rocked," until the tenor man locks his eyes on Dean as "a madman who not only understood but cared and wanted to understand more and much more than there was, and they began dueling for this."

Kerouac, who spoke the French-Canadian dialect joual as his first language and came to English through its foreign sounds and rhythms, remained entranced by the possibility of communicating through sounds, as if they channeled a voice beyond language. At the end of *Big Sur*, he composed a long poem of sea sounds. His greatest distrust was for craft. "I worried," he wrote in 1948, "because it begins to be vaguely apparent to me that I can write without 'spiritual torment,' as others have done, and with artistic successfulness. Artistic is one thing, connected with the world; and *spiritual* is another, connected with me and my demented heaven." He preached against silencing this voice through even judicious revision.

Dean's gibberish, then, becomes richer as it breaks further away from conventional sense, toward glossolalia. It communicates as shout and rhythm, casting the exact spell parents feared first from demon jazz, then rock or hip-hop. It drives young men from their parents' homes and possesses young women to lie back without shame. Dean has no trouble communicating in Mexico even though he speaks no Spanish. Like Tolstoy's happiness, his blowing is universal.

There is simply no connection between men and time. Men are only involved in space and place. My father for instance is no further from me now than New Hampshire. . . . Cause-and-effect is also a prurience of mind and soul, because it pettishly demands surface answers to bottomless matters.

—Journals, October 1949

ON THE ROAD'S structure, as Warren Tallman has pointed out, is a jazz form. Instead of building toward a resolution, like a European novel, Kerouac's tale circles back on itself, like a jazz musician working successive choruses on the same changes. There is no linear progression. After the first journey gets Sal on the road, the next three take Sal and Dean through roughly the same paces, like variations on a theme, usually ending with a sore parting and beginning anew with the urge to move. The fifth journey adds a coda.

For half a century, *On the Road* has tempted filmmakers with its smorgasbord of sex, sound and action—most recently, the Brazilian-born director Walter Salles Jr. But so far, none has made it into production. The story doesn't really lend itself to the screen. The action repeats, the climaxes pop up without warning and go by without consequence. The events of one journey don't carry over to another, and even within journeys there is little continuity from one episode to the next. Kerouac could have added another trip or taken one away. No wonder Ginsberg thought it needed an ending, or Jerry Wald of 20th Century Fox wanted Dean to die in a car crash. Movies don't flow this way.

But jazz does. A jazz soloist cuts a circular path rather than a linear one: He'll pick up a riff, reverse it, pull it apart, put it back together and return to it to launch anew. He can blow for a short spell or a long one. When he runs out of ideas, all he has to do is make it back to where he started. And even when he's done, the tune isn't finished; it's just waiting for him or someone else to pick it up and reinvent it. Instead of defining an idea as a classical composer would, jazz musicians continually explore it from different angles, as if rotating a gem to let the light pour through it in new ways. A tune like "Ornithology" or "My Favorite Things" becomes the sum of all versions.

Kerouac picks up this line early in *On the Road*. Carlo and Dean are in their marathon libidinal mind-meld in Denver, and Carlo says there's "just one last thing" he wants to know. Sal, who has been listening quietly, interrupts: "That last thing is what you can't get, Carlo. Nobody can get to that last thing. We keep on living in hopes of catching it once and for all." On first read, the line seems to be about death. But in a book that is obsessed with concepts of time, the line also signals the nature of the narrative to come: It will not build to a final climax and denouement but will deal in momentary flashes of illumination, episodically. In other words, it will move like the road, or a jazz ensemble. As Sal says, "we had longer ways to go. But no matter, the road is life."

In the late Chicago hours, George Shearing leads the boys to this same lesson in musical form, hammering a solo that leaves them sighing. "There ain't nothin left after that," one musician says, until finally they decide to blow anyway. "Something would come of it yet," Sal says. "There's always more, a little further—it never ends. They sought to find new phrases after Shearing's explorations; they tried hard. They writhed and twisted and blew. Every now and then a clear harmonic cry gave new suggestions of a tune that would someday be the only tune in the world and would raise men's souls to joy. They found it, they lost, they wrestled for it, they found it again, they laughed, they moaned—and Dean sweated at the table and told them to go, go, go. At nine o'clock in the morning everybody—musicians, girls in slacks, bartenders, and the one little skinny, unhappy trombonist—staggered out of the club into the great roar of Chicago day to sleep until the wild bop night again."

On the Road, similarly, is organized as a series of new beginnings. The wild bop night, which restarts every twenty-four hours, leads not toward a final statement but to the creation of a moment, a process that is never complete. As Dean says, "You and I, Sal, we'd dig the whole world with a car like this because, man, the road must eventually lead to the whole world. Ain't nowhere else it can go—right?"

Each journey begins like the tune that Shearing's musicians take up, with a germ that might raise men's souls to joy. Their repetition is part of the form. There's always more, a little further. Like a musician revisiting familiar chords, Sal finds himself revisiting places from past trips, stacking their meanings vertically rather than horizontally. "I was crisscrossing the old map again," he says, "same place Marylou and I had held hands on a snowy morning in 1949, and where was Marylou now? 'Blow!' said Dean in a dream and I guess he was dreaming of Frisco jazz and maybe Mexican mambo to come." As the bop night connects distances, Sal's travels connect time.

Writing in Jazz Time

Kerouac once compared his Duluoz legend, which was then up to seven volumes, to Proust "done on the run, a Running Proust." He praised Proust as "an old teahead of time." But his time is different from Proust's. Instead of past remembrances determining the present, Sal's past and present are variations on the same themes, neither subordinate to the other. He organizes time the way a jazzman organizes successive choruses—each revisiting familiar terrain, adding the new and revivifying the old. Where Dean ropes time to a schedule, in parody of the work world, Sal's time loops back on itself, like his travels. The eastern landscape contains the wilds of the colonial frontier; the owner of the fish-and-chips joint is Sal's mother from the Dickensian past; Sal's postwar America contains the goodness of Whitman's. Sal's lesson about time is to understand these pairings simultaneously rather than sequentially, to make one shine through the other.

Because Sal is always in the moment, he has no sense of proportion. Every gig he goes to is the best ever, every laugh is "positively and finally the one greatest laugh in all this world." Everything Sal experiences is bigger than the words he has for it, leaving the language overwhelmed, and asking the reader to put it back together, reenacting Sal's enthusiasm in the process. Even ordinary experiences are exceptional because they're his, and surely no one ever experienced them quite the same before.

Kerouac, too, was perpetually enthusiastic about whatever was at hand, in part because he didn't analyze his experiences, Carolyn Cassady said. "I think he responded to everything emotionally first, and that's why he will say with some very heavy opinion one minute and then two minutes later he's just as adamant about the opposite views, and we could never pin him down as to what it is he really believed, because it changed every five minutes." It was not just egomania for Kerouac, a barely published writer, to compare his manuscript-in-progress to Tolstoy or Joyce, because within the moment his manuscript was the only one that existed for him—so of course it was the best.

We've all had this experience with a piece of music: For the time you're in it, it's the best thing you've ever heard because it's the only music that exists. What other music is there? But for the most part we live under more oppressive continuities. Sal lives this way all the time. In stepping across chronological time, he invites readers to ditch the causes and effects we suffer under: that we should study hard, get a job, move up the ladder, or sacrifice now for the eventual hereafter—*feh!* Kerouac rejected these hierarchies. He laid this out to a baffled crowd at Hunter College: "The Lord said that the attainment of enlightenment is neither to be considered a high state nor a low state. Everybody equally attains it. Because everybody equally knows, as Allen Ginsberg says, that lightning strikes in the blue sky." Since revelation happens at the drop of a hat, there's no point studying for it, nor pretending you're closer than somebody else.

Even nuclear apocalypse is a cyclical event, not a final one. On the trip to Mexico, Sal and Dean move vertically through time, into a past that is premodern, and into an image of a postnuclear future. Mexico is both of these—a jazz way of life opening up to Sal at last, a tune with infinite variations. Mexico is a version of Sal's America displaced in time, or of the lost city of Atlantis, the journey's mythic starting point. All are variations on the same theme of destruction and redemption. In the "great and final wild uninhibited Fellahin-childlike city that we knew we would find at the end of the road," Sal realizes what George Shearing's sidemen learned on the bandstand: that there is no end of the road, because "nothing ever ended." The time is *always* now. What other time is there?

Jazz provides Kerouac with a way of engaging death as part of the continuum of life, ever present, rather than an end. Knowing time means knowing that it doesn't end, it just circles back on itself, like Parker on an infinite jam. Ee-yah, indeed.

Sal's Blues (Slight Return)

I recognize that this is a very limited way to discuss jazz. You could make the same claims for Kerouac's writing without invoking this holy mantle. Most people who compare novels to jazz are writers of jacket copy. At any rate, Kerouac was a jazz romantic, not an adept. Kenneth Rexroth, an early advocate for the Beats, dismissed Kerouac's treatment of jazz as sentimental and patronizing, steeped in the same "primitive" stereotypes used by more conventional racists. "Now there are two things Jack knows nothing about," he wrote—"jazz and Negroes. His idea of jazz is that it is savage drums and screaming horns around the jungle fire while the missionary soup comes to boil."

Rexroth comes on strong—he believed Kerouac helped engineer an affair between his wife and Robert Creeley—but his criticism is on target. Kerouac's depictions of improvisation, always "spontaneous," allow little room for the musicians' conscious thought, and he ignores the discipline and skill that go into even the most visceral blowing. His club scenes pass over the folks who just want to meet girls or unwind after work. And he hurt his cause with an essay that described Lionel Hampton, the vibraphonist, leaping into a crowd with his sax.

But the jazz lessons Kerouac applied to his own work were more nuanced, especially with *On the Road*. Written and rewritten over a four-year period, and revised after, it is a book of the woodshed. Like the musicians he admired, he built his performance from riffs and ideas honed over a long period of time, written in his letters and notebooks. He didn't just blow off the

Woodshedding

For all his self-generated rep for spontaneous prose, Kerouac worked out his riffs in letters and journals before committing them to manuscript, in the same way musicians hone their chops in the woodshed before blowing them fresh onstage. Take Carlo's famous inquisition, "What is the meaning of this voyage to New York? What kind of sordid business are you on now? I mean, man, whither goest thou? Whither goes thou, America, in thy shiny car at night?" The line is an accusation, and Sal has no answer to it. But when it first appeared in Kerouac's 1949 journals, it was a romp: "Neal and I and Louanne talking of the value of life as we speed along, in such thoughts as 'Whither goest thou America in thy shiny car at night?' and in the mere fact that we're together under such rainy circumstances talking heart to heart. Seldom had I been so glad of life." That May, Kerouac quoted the journal passage to Ed White, adding the sentence, "Telling ghost stories even." The following year, in a letter from Mexico to John Holmes, he attributed the line to the Great Walking Saint, who "stands on the side of Highway 66 looking at all the cars that pass, saying 'Whither Goest Thou?'" In a January 1951 letter to Ginsberg, he changed vehicles, asking, apropos of nothing, "Whither goest thou, O America, in thy frantic truck at night? Whee!" Three months later, in the scroll draft, Ginsberg's inquisition is trimmed to a repeated "Whither goest thou?" without America or vehicle. The final version, to Kerouac's credit, combines the best from all.

top of his head. What he got from jazz was a way of seeing and recording in the moment, moving like the fast cars and faster atoms of the postwar years.

As early as 1949, Kerouac told Ed White of a change in his

approach to writing. "For me," he said, "the truth is rushing from moment to moment incomprehensible, ungraspable, but terribly *clear*." Artists in other disciplines were already starting to capture this motion, in the action painting of the abstract expressionist crowd downtown or the quicksilver bop improvisation uptown, which replaced set pieces with blowing that only suggested the structures underneath. Jackson Pollock made his first drip canvas the previous year, capturing the movement of creation in the work itself. Kerouac would eventually dig it all. He drank with the painters at the Cedar Tavern and hit the spots uptown, and through his friend Jerry Newman, a record producer, he had the honor of Dizzy Gillespie titling an arrangement "Kerouac."

Kerouac felt novels were not keeping up; they were all problems and solutions. To capture the truth, he told White, he had to begin by making his life his art. "I can't describe these things logically," he wrote. "The only possible way to suggest what I mean is to re-arrange life in an artwork that will demonstrate what I mean and what I think we all mean." *On the Road* is his first step in this direction. Marking the development in his 1948 journal, he wrote that his words "get away from me in a trance of writing as I type along. I've always been afraid of trying this—this may be it. This may be the greatest 'break' in my writing since last November." Yet even then he was years away from the break that freed him to write the scroll draft.

Readers have long taken Kerouac at his word that he wrote *On the Road* in three weeks in April 1951, banging the keys the way Dean drove, without deliberation or self-censorship. This impression, which he cultivated, remains the essential image of Kerouac as a writer. It led to Truman Capote's famous dismissal, "That isn't writing; it's typing." The myth suited his work: To capture the noise and speed of his social life, he created a writing regimen that translated these to a solo performance. His cloister was as noisy and sweaty as his drawing room.

But recent access to many of his letters and journals shows that he was composing scenes and descriptions well before the scroll marathon—testing them, revising them and saving every version for later reference. Late in life, after many readers had stopped caring, Kerouac described his writing practice, which he was still learning with *On the Road*: "You think out what actually happened, you tell friends long stories about it, you mull it over in your mind, you connect it together at leisure, then when the time comes to pay the rent again, you force yourself to sit at the typewriter, or at the writing notebook, and get it over with as fast as you can . . . and there's no harm in that, because you've got the whole story lined up." So there is speed but also practice, deliberation and revision. A month after he finished the scroll draft, he wrote to Cassady, "Of course since Apr. 22 I've been typing and revising. Thirty days on that. Will be my routine."

Much of the Kerouac myth stems from a 1953 essay called "The Essentials of Spontaneous Prose," which he wrote at the suggestion of Ginsberg and Burroughs as a blueprint for future writers. "If possible," he advised, "write 'without consciousness' in semi-trance (as Yeats' later 'trance writing') allowing subconscious to admit in own uninhibited interesting necessary and so 'modern' language what conscious art would censor, and write excitedly, swiftly, with writing-or-typing-cramps, in accordance (as from center to periphery) with laws of orgasm, Reich's 'beclouding of consciousness.'" Never mind that this sentence is a good argument against spontaneous composition; for Kerouac the process became a grail. The impulse to improve a sentence, he argued, was an affront to your holy calling, and was rooted in shame. Why let your internalized high school English teacher edit what God gave you?

But Kerouac wrote this essay two years *after* the scroll draft, about methods he developed only later. *On the Road* is not spontaneous prose. He remained unsatisfied with the novel, and told Elbert Lenrow after its success, "when I wrote ON THE ROAD I really didn't think much of it and still inclined to think little of it. Yes, the Myth of the Rainy Night [*Doctor Sax*] is writ, and that's the book, that's the book I have which I'm proud to say to YOU is writ." Some critics have seconded Kerouac's emotion, deeming *On the Road* a prelude to Kerouac's more adventurous experiments—or, as Tim Hunt has suggested, a second-to-last draft of the novel that was eventually published as *Visions of Cody*. "[T]his is all like bop," Kerouac mused in the latter book, "we're getting to it indirectly and too late but completely from every angle except the angle we all don't know."

This is a matter of taste; I find large stretches of *Visions of Cody*, as when he strays too far from narrative, self-indulgent and tedious. Part of *On the Road*'s kick is the tension that comes of being *in between,* dashing ahead of readers' formal expectations but accommodating them at the same time. Its naïveté matches Sal's, taking on the big questions of existence in a form that aspires to the mainstream. He worked hard on his spontaneity. This paradox spreads from the prose to the characters and back. However headlong their steps into the unknown, Sal and Dean are traditionalists, looking to connect with old forms, not slay them. In their lament for lost fathers, they are creatures of nostalgia as well as New Men. What Kerouac got from Wolfe and Proust was the persistence of memory, and what he got from jazz was the freedom to pull memory apart, to play variations on its changes. Sal is learning to tell the story in front of us—a little square, like us, but pushed by Dean and the players on the bandstand.

Ann Douglas, considering Kerouac's whole body of work, called it "the most extensive experiment in language and literary form undertaken by an American writer of his generation." Measured by sheer volume of words, this is probably true. But this was not Kerouac's intent with *On the Road*, any more than Charlie Parker set out to create the free jazz of the sixties. Like the bop musicians of Parker's generation, who learned their craft in conventional swing bands, Kerouac stood at the precipice of greater freedom but did not yet go there. He merely suggested that it was possible. The jazz in *On the Road*, ultimately, lies not in "spontaneous prose" but in its moments of unnamed ecstasy, accessible as Dexter Gordon and Wardell Gray in "The Hunt," but still not cleaned up for proper society. These moments are like the book's revelations, fleeting. But they define time and space and meaning for the characters, and give the book its chockalocka rhythm. They aren't the last word on jazz because, as the musicians learn from Shearing, "There's always more, a little further—it never ends."

Sal learns the same lesson from Mississippi Gene, the wise old hobo. "I hope you get where you're going, and be happy when you do," Sal tells him. Gene replies, "I always make out and move along one way or the other." This is a jazz song as pure as any—laconic, improvised and never finished. Like Sal, it is drawn to both freedom and home, and to the bewildering, senseless road in between. On the road as on the bandstand, form and freedom aren't opposites, they're complements, equal parts of a tune that's still working itself out, one solo at a time.

Visions of Sal

The Holy Goofs

Ghosts

Visions

I've never written about Jesus? In other words, you're an insane
phony who comes to my house . . . and . . . all I *write about* is Jesus.
—Remark to Ted Berrigan, 1968

WHEN Kerouac came down from Desolation Peak in
the North Cascade Mountains in 1956, after two months of
solitary fire spotting, he ran around San Francisco with his hair
uncombed and a crucifix around his neck, a gift from Gregory
Corso. By this time, Kerouac had deepened in his Catholic faith,
mixing it with his more recent enthusiasm for Buddhism. He
wore the crucifix outside his shirt to the famous group photo
shoot for *Mademoiselle*'s article about the San Francisco
renaissance. When the photos were reprinted with reviews of *On
the Road* the following year, he complained about a conspicuous
pattern of cropping: Every publication except the *New York Times*,
he noted, chopped the crucifix from his breast, "as though it
were something distasteful."

The disappearing crucifix was just the first sign of how the
book's religious intentions would go over. Kerouac called the
novel "a story about 2 Catholic buddies roaming the country in
search of God. And we found him. I found him in the sky, in
Market Street San Francisco (those 2 visions), and Dean had God

149

sweating out of his forehead all the way." But despite the characters' repeated references to God, salvation and redemption, the book's religious dimension has been overshadowed by the image of two wild and crazy guys. While hipsters have approved Kerouac's self-taught Buddhism, they have largely ignored his devotion to the cross.

Kerouac's Catholicism is an elusive strand in his writing. He was an altar boy at St. Jean Baptiste Cathedral in Lowell, and at one point was considered a future candidate for the priesthood. The French-Canadian Catholic Church leaned toward the severe writings of Cornelius Otto Jansen, which focused on original sin and the depravity of human nature, but Kerouac was attracted more to the figure of the suffering, liberating Christ than to church discipline or doctrine. As a child he identified his late older brother, Gerard, with Christ. He was an early "cafeteria Catholic," picking what he wanted, including a personal relationship with Jesus rather than an institutional one. Though he stopped attending mass at age 14, he began writing about angels and Jesus later in high school, and his adult notebooks are filled with religious drawings, prayers and meditations. His studies in Buddhism, which sprang from reading Thoreau, took place largely after he wrote *On the Road*.

To anyone who would listen, Kerouac professed that he and his friends constituted "the Second Religiousness that Oswald Spengler prophesied for the West," citing as evidence their "beatific indifference to things that are Caesar's . . . a tiredness of that, and a yearning for, a regret for, the transcendent value, or 'God,' again." His definition of literature was a "tale told for companionship and to teach something religious, of religious reverence," and he lamented that his teachings typically got lost in Beat mystique and controversy. All he could do, he wrote, was to fill his novels with "the preachment of universal kindness, which hysterical critics have failed to notice beneath frenetic activity of my true-story novels about the 'beat' generation.—Am actually not 'beat' but strange solitary crazy Catholic mystic."

Church of the Road

Here lies a paradox of *On the Road*: The book that Kerouac envisioned is far more pious and oppressive than the one he actually delivered. Kerouac bored friends with his Catholic and Buddhist enthusiasms. "I shall . . . preach (if I can) in my work," he wrote in his 1949 journals, and when he described himself, it was as a character you'd never want to go on the road with: "I am he who watches the Lamb; I am he who has adopted the Sorrows; I am he, John L. Kerouac, the Serious, the Severe, the Stubborn, the Unappeased." If he'd written the novel he intended, we wouldn't be thinking about it today. The book's virtues are made possible in part by its failures. A Catholic without a church, he produced the form of a religious allegory without the inconvenient doctrine.

Kerouac's Church of the Road, in fact, is uncommonly genial in its commandments. Premarital sex, drugs, divorce, prostitution, homosexuality, devil music—all fit neatly into its gospel. Stealing cars? No problem. Betraying your friends? It's the way to sainthood. This church demands no tithes, meatless Fridays or service to others. It has no sermons to sit through or scriptures to study. Its hymns are bop. The only requirement is unblemished self-absorption. In Galatea Dunkel's scolding soliloquy, after Dean has left Camille in San Francisco, she sings the credentials of the new hipster saint: "For years now you haven't had any sense of responsibility for anyone," she tells Dean. "You've done so many awful things I don't know what to say to you. . . . Not only that but you're silly about it. It never occurs to you that life is serious and there are people trying to make something decent out of it instead of just goofing all the time."

Dean simply rubs his belly and licks his lips. This is his canonical moment, when Sal realizes his friend's true status as the Holy Goof. Dean is "ragged and broken and idiotic," Sal says, "his bony mad face covered with sweat and throbbing veins, saying, 'Yes, yes, yes,' as though tremendous revelations were pouring into him all the time now, and I am convinced they were, and the others suspected as much and were frightened. . . . Bitterness, recriminations, advice, morality, sadness—everything was behind him, and ahead of him was the ragged and ecstatic joy of pure being." All Dean says is, "Ah, man, don't worry, everything is perfect and fine."

Every church should cut this much slack.

But if *On the Road* lacks a cudgel of "thou shalt not," it is structured as a spiritual search, for which the heroes willingly undergo poverty, bad food and social ostracism, to say nothing of sexual excess and the nightmares caused by uncured weed. They seek and experience visions, encounter ghosts and engage the fundamental religious questions of death and the afterlife. From the moment Sal leaves home, following Dean as "a new kind of American saint," Kerouac frames their travels as a holy quest and relates them in religious language. The thunderclaps at Bear Mountain "put the fear of God in me," Sal says, setting the tone for the adventures to follow. On these journeys, he promises, there will be "girls, visions, everything."

Where Goethe's Faust, a child of the Enlightenment, sought wisdom through his own rational study, Sal and Dean are products of the Enlightenment's failures—of Hiroshima, Auschwitz and Levittown—seeking wisdom only through revelation. They are looking for the incomprehensible, which even storytellers and con artists cannot capture in words. "And of course now no one can tell us that there is no God," Dean says at the start of the second journey. "You remember, Sal, when I first came to New York and I wanted Chad King to teach me about Nietzsche"—in other words, that God was dead. "You see how long ago? Everything is fine, God exists, we know time. . . . And not only that but we both understand that I couldn't have time to explain why I know and you know God exists."

The boys begin their travels not as a quest for secular knowledge but a rejection of it. Writing twelve years after *The Wizard of Oz* movie, Kerouac seems determined to show that the man in the booth really *is* a wizard—that the world is mysterious, supernatural, impervious to scientific or rational analysis. He was looking, he wrote to himself, for "a purpose in eternity, something to decide on from which I'll never deviate now in whatever dark existence or other follows. . . . Why should I want this?—Because there isn't enough here on earth to want, or that is, not a single thing here exists that I do want. . . . [R]eason and the body of facts, science and truth, do not make me feel, and do not bridge eternity, and in fact choke me like stale, close air."

Accordingly, Sal abandons his map; Dean rejects the tradition of "geometry and geometrical systems of thinking" that has served since the Greeks. When they meet two Jesuit students, Sal dismisses them with one of the book's best lines: "They were full of corny quips and Eastern college talk and had nothing on their bird-beans except a lot of ill-understood Aquinas for stuffing for their pepper. Dean and I paid absolutely no attention to them." Instead Sal recognizes the emerging sainthood in Dean, which is most holy when least coherent. "He was out of his mind with real belief," Sal says. "There was nothing clear about the things he said, but what he meant to say was somehow made pure and clear." Dean is on the way to his destiny as the Holy Goof, a bop riff on the Christian tradition of the holy fool or fool for Christ.

Fools for Christ

In the New Testament, the apostle Paul defines an earlier tribe of holy goofs. Like Sal and Dean, Paul and the apostles are poor, nomadic and scorned by proper religious folk. "We are fools for Christ's sake," he lectures the recalcitrant Christians of Corinth,

> but ye are wise in Christ; we are weak, but ye are strong; ye are honorable, but we are despised.
>
> Even unto this present hour we both hunger, and thirst, and are naked, and are buffeted, and have no certain dwelling place;
>
> and labor, working with our own hands: being reviled, we bless; being persecuted, we suffer it:
>
> being defamed, we entreat: we are made as the filth of the world, and are the offscouring of all things unto this day.

Paul's holy fools are naked, homeless and outcast—perfect role models for Sal and Dean, who become "ragged and dirty as if we had lived off locust." Both parties, as Paul says, "are made a spectacle unto the world, and to angels, and to men."

One mark of the holy fool is the compulsion to travel. John Saward, in his study *Perfect Fools: Folly for Christ's Sake in Catholic and Orthodox Spirituality*, describes the fool's wandering as "a way of practising self-abasement, for unlike the Pilgrim to the Holy

Places, who has a definite earthly destination, the exile or pereg-rinus has a dangerously vagabond air and so is despised; he is a voluntary outlaw. Peregrination is a way of imitating, and grow-ing in union with, the humiliated Christ." In the biblical sense, then, *On the Road* is a fool's mission, embodying a Christian para-dox: Travel is both a reminder of man's expulsion from Eden and an expression of Christlike humility and sacrifice. For Sal and Dean, as for fallen man, the road is a penance, not an adventure.

The poverty of holy fools—whether Paul's or Kerouac's—is not a Woody Guthrie romance, meant to shame the rich or arouse the egalitarian. Instead it is a pointed type of powerless-ness. Like Paul, Kerouac's nomads want knowledge that comes without power, since the combination of knowledge and power has proven so destructive. Paul commanded the Corinthians to abandon their learning for holy ignorance: "If any man among you seemeth to be wise in this world," he wrote, "let him be-come a fool, that he may be wise. For the wisdom of the world is foolishness with God." Foolishness shifts attention away from "problems," which have rational solutions, to spiritual matters, which do not.

Highway Apostles

The holy figures Sal and Dean meet on the road, like Paul's apostles, speak a strange language that might be mistaken for babble by the unblessed. Some are jazz musicians, talking in the EE-yah of their horns; some are Mexican Indians, speaking Span-ish that the guys don't understand. On the second journey, after the traffic fine forces them to pick up hitchhikers for gas money, they meet a perfect fool in a Virginia town called Testament. "The man was a ragged, bespectacled mad type," Sal says, "walk-ing along reading a paperbacked muddy book he'd found in a culvert by the road. He got in the car and went right on reading; he was incredibly filthy and covered with scabs. He said his name was Hyman Solomon and that he walked all over the USA, knocking and sometimes kicking at Jewish doors and demanding money: 'Give me money to eat, I am a Jew.'" (This seems an unlikely gig in midcentury Virginia, but never mind.) When they ask what he is reading he doesn't know. "He didn't bother to look at the title page. He was only looking at the words, as though he had found the real Torah where it belonged, in the wilderness."

Hyman is both a biblical figure and a storyteller, carrying the real Torah of the wilderness: He is a fool and a writer. Like Sal, he can't decipher the prophecies he has been given (according to Kerouac's journals, the book was actually a detective story, which is far less mysterious). But Hyman plies his trade dutifully. Instead of fleeing his poverty he receives alms for it. Sal's mission, similarly, is to figure out the prophecy he is meant to deliver. Through Solomon he sees that revelation—the real Torah—is in the wilderness, "where it belonged," indecipherable even for the people who carry it. Sal's wilderness is the road. He recalls the promise he felt at the beginning of the book, that "somewhere along the line a pearl would be handed to me." Now he and Dean see their reward coming within reach. "He and I suddenly saw the whole country like an oyster for us to open," Sal says; "and the pearl was there, the pearl was there."

On the surface, Sal seems to present Dean as the book's holy fool, and himself as a passive observer. The Russian scholar Elena Volkova has objected to calling Dean a holy fool, or *iurodi-vyi*, because he is such an unholy glutton. But Sal applies more forgiving criteria for sainthood. As Kerouac spelled out in *Visions of Cody*, his friend is "entirely irresponsible to the point of wild example and purgation for us to learn and not have to go through, like the pale criminal genius who kills our old suburban queen to show us it can be done and doesn't have to be done, and Jesus crucified." By designating Dean the Holy Goof, Sal absolves himself and others from responsibility for him. There's no need to protect Dean from his destructive idiocy because it is the basis of his holiness. "His bandage was getting dirtier all the time," Sal says; "it began to flop and unroll. I suddenly realized that Dean, by virtue of his enormous series of sins, was becoming the Idiot, the Imbecile, the Saint of the lot." The more nonsensical or ragged Dean gets, and the more he alienates even his friends, the closer he gets to the Pauline ideal.

His holiness is apparent in his sweat, which creates a brotherhood of idiocy. A dozen times Sal mentions Dean's perspiration. "It's my contention that a man who can sweat fantastically for the flesh is also capable of sweating fantastically for the spirit," Kerouac wrote to the theology student Carroll Brown. "THERE IS NO OTHER WAY OUT FOR THE HOLY MAN: HE MUST SWEAT FOR GOD."

The Other Idiot

But *On the Road* is as much about Sal's descent (or ascent) into foolishness; Dean merely plows the way. From the beginning, Sal is the odd man out, shambling behind Carlo and Dean's dingledodies. "I was a lout compared," he says, "I couldn't keep up with them." Kerouac harps on Sal's early embarrassments and his friends' mockery. After beginning his first journey with the humiliation in Bear Mountain, Sal amuses Remi Boncoeur in California with his rube innocence. "I had just come through the little fishing village of Sausalito," Sal recounts, "and the first thing I said was, 'There must be a lot of Italians in Sausalito.'

"'There must be a lot of Italians in Sausalito!' [Remi] shouted at the top of his lungs. 'Aaaaah!' He pounded himself, he fell on the bed, he almost rolled on the floor. 'Did you hear what Paradise said? There must be a lot of Italians in Sausalito? Aaaah-haaa! Hoo! Wow! Whee!' He got red as a beet, laughing. 'Oh, you slay me, Paradise, you're the funniest man in the world, and here you are, you finally got here, he came in through the window, you saw him, Lee Ann, he followed instructions and came in through the window. Aaaah! Hooo!'"

Jane Lee, in Louisiana, gives him a cooler but equally mocking welcome. "'Isn't that a fire or something over there?'" she asks him. "We both looked toward the sun.

"'You mean the sun?'

"'Of course I don't mean the sun. . . .' Jane snuffed down her nose. 'Same old Paradise.'"

Kerouac occasionally referred to himself as an idiot or imbecile, usually to signify his feelings of martyrdom. "We will be justified in Heaven," he wrote to Ginsberg. "In the living world, I am like an Imbecile." By the time he wrote *Big Sur* in 1961, he called his narrator "the last poor holy fool," which he now defined as "a special solitary angel sent down as a messenger from Heaven to tell everybody or show everybody by example that their peeking society was actually the Satanic Society and they were all on the wrong track."

Dean's foolishness ultimately leaves him cold and ragged on a New York street, with no hope that the next revelation will make things any easier. He has to go on suffering as proof of his visions. But for Sal, the visions have an outlet in his writing. Though he can't explain the revelations, he transposes them into literary form. Kerouac defended his high-speed writing methods as a way of freeing foolish wisdom from a writer's rational tendency to self-censor. "What a man most wishes to hide, revise, and un-say, is precisely what Literature is waiting and bleeding for," he told Cowley. "I foresee a new literature on account of this—but it's hard, it's paradoxical, i.e., it's taken me all my life to learn to write what I actually think—*by not thinking*." The results are prose that imitates the workings of a mind in motion. "I looked up out of the dark swirl of my mind," Sal says in Mexico, "and I knew I was on a bed eight thousand feet above sea level, on a roof of the world, and I knew that I had lived a whole life and many others in the poor atomistic husk of my flesh, and I had all the dreams."

This is the germ of an idea, caught as it is forming and gone by the start of the next sentence. At his best, Kerouac extracts the fool's thoughts before the wiser man can polish or correct them. He makes a case for knowledge as it exists in nature: unrefined and disconnected, disorderly. For all the fool's piety, its role is an impious one, to impose chaos on the illusion of order. In other words, to tell the messy truth.

[M]ore and more as I grow older I see the beautiful dream of life expanding till it is much more important than gray life itself—a dark, red dream the color of the cockatoo. Night, like a balm, soothes dumb wounds of prickly day-dark & rainy night!

I am grown more mystic than ever now.

—Journal, July 4, 1949

THE big kahuna for any god-aspiring novelist is the question of death. *What's going to happen to us when we die?* Sal, who asks this question directly of Bull Lee, receives answers from various ghosts, spirits, angels, dreams and weed-induced visions. In a novel set in circular jazz time, where the past coexists with the present, Bull's initial answer to Sal—*you're just dead, that's all*—is unsatisfying even to Bull. "Mankind will someday realize that we are actually in contact with the dead and with the other world, whatever it is," he tells Sal, amending his view; "right now we could predict, if we only exerted enough mental will, what is going to happen within the next hundred years and be able to take steps to avoid all kinds of catastrophes. When a man dies he undergoes a mutation in his brain that we know nothing about now but which will be very clear someday if scientists get on the ball. The bastards right now are only interested in seeing if they can blow up the world." In Bull's view, the dead are with us always; the bastards, too.

If not for its other ambitions, *On the Road* might be read as a ghost story, peopled with apparitions both living and dead. From the moment Sal leaves home, he peers behind the membrane that separates the natural world from the supernatural, starting at the cheap hotel in Des Moines where he wakes up not knowing who he is. "I wasn't scared," he says; "I was just somebody else, some stranger, and my whole life was a haunted life, the life of a ghost." For fifteen strange seconds, he is on the other side of the membrane, and he realizes that the side he has been living on is the side of ghosts. The next world, it seems, isn't where you go in the future, but runs side by side with this one. He is barely a bus ride from home and already he has peeked over at the other side.

Almost a year before the scroll draft, Kerouac wrote a version of this scene in his journal as the opening for the novel, which he was then calling *Gone on the Road*. These notes offer more detail about the supernatural experience. The scene prompts a "change in my life that led to the events I implore God to help arrange in my mind so that I may bring them to light." It begins with a recognition that he is growing old and will die. "In a proud dream of life, like life after death of an angel that has died," he wrote, "I lay as if revealed, in bed, to a mighty gaze that became, in time, more personal and merciful and assumed a voice, reproachful, even friendly and complaining in tone like the voice of a dead ancestor."

It's an odd image for a first-person narrator: As he looks at himself from the outside, he becomes aware of another "mighty gaze" also looking at him. In detaching from himself, he is acting out literally his role as a narrator—a ghostlike function that allows him to operate in two worlds, each with its own laws. The narrator in the scene is a character, a ghost of a character, a displaced observer and the one telling the story. The line connecting the mortal world and the spirit world leads him to that between storytellers and their subjects.

Though Kerouac abandoned most of the scene by the time of the scroll draft, the book's characters remain in contact with ghosts and spirits. As Sal and Dean bomb around the continent, their most exotic travels are metaphysical, crossing borders of time, death and the supernatural. Sometimes the ghosts they meet are fellow travelers, like the Ghost of the Susquehanna; sometimes they are voices from the beyond, like the tip passed by Sal's father at the bookie joint in Louisiana; and sometimes they are elusive presences never seen, like Old Dean or the Times Square hustler Elmer Hassel, who haunts the book from coast to coast without ever making an appearance. Sal and Dean's search for their fathers is a search for origins, but also for endings—and for the connections between the beginning and end of life's journey.

Sal starts to make these connections after his first trip west, returning home with a changed understanding of life and death. Looking in vain for Hassel, he realizes, "I had traveled eight thousand miles around the American continent and I was back on Times Square; and right in the middle of rush hour, too, seeing with my innocent road-eyes the absolute madness and fantastic hoorair of New York with its millions and millions hustling forever for a buck among themselves, the mad dream—grabbing, taking, giving, sighing, dying, just so they could be buried in those awful cemetery cities beyond Long Island City." The conventional view that death is what follows and crowns life, he decides, demeans both.

Ghosts are a matter-of-fact presence in *On the Road*, no more remarkable than the dreams or pop cultural images that also haunt the travelers. On the second journey, Ed Dunkel tells Sal of seeing his dead mother in a Utah ranch, then of meeting his own ghost in midtown Manhattan. "Last night I walked clear down to Times Square and just as I arrived I suddenly realized I was a ghost—it was my ghost walking on the sidewalk," he says. Like Sal's briefly glanced ghost life, Ed's ghosts coexist beside

Old Man Sal

Kerouac was twenty-five when he began the first journey, twenty-nine when he wrote the scroll draft and thirty-five when the book was published. Sal, on the other hand, is of indeterminate age, leaving only a few misleading hints. "Oh, I'm a college boy!" he tells Terry, and, later, to a cop: "I'm a friend on a two-week vacation from college." In fact, Kerouac left Columbia College in 1941 and took only occasional classes at The New School. In a pre-scroll draft he took note of his advancing years: "And I had grown old," he wrote. "I stared in the mirror to see the damage of the slob, grieving, all-grieving at the sight of it, astonished at the suffering face I saw, fairly horrified by the drawn, hooded eye that looked at me." But in the final version, he spared himself this indignity, creating a gap between his image and his age that was exacerbated by publishing delays. As he wrote in *Big Sur*, "all over America highschool and college kids thinking 'Jack Duluoz is 26 years old and on the road all the time hitch hiking' while there I am almost 40 years old, bored and jaded in a roomette bunk."

his more conventional doings. Ed doesn't seem to get much from his ghosts; they're just there, showing the characters that this other world exists. Nor does Sal ask for further explanation—such as, um, *how did you know?*—even as Ed mentions his ghost for the third time. Why ask? The main thing is to recognize the inexplicable. Rational explication would only gum things up.

Chasing the Shroud

Ed's talk of ghosts sets off something in Sal. "Just about that time a strange thing began to haunt me," he says. "It was this: I had forgotten something. There was a decision that I was about to make before Dean showed up, and now it was driven clear out of my mind but still hung on the tip of my mind's tongue. I kept snapping my fingers, trying to remember it. I even mentioned it. And I couldn't even tell if it was a real decision or just a thought I had forgotten. It haunted and flabbergasted me, made me sad. It had to do somewhat with the Shrouded Traveler."

Kerouac was fascinated with a recurring dream figure he called the Shrouded Traveler or Hooded Wayfarer. He believed that dreams were a form of memory, immaterial but just as real. "When a man dreams," he told Cassady in their pre-scroll flurry of confessional letters, "he can't pluck his dream-image from the air that surrounds his bed; no, on the contrary, the image and the whole material in which it sits, is already in his mind; where did it come from; it comes from that part of his brain which has stored up a subconscious vision of an actual experience. . . . [A]ll dreams come from visions of experience; they are released because they are already there in the mind."

In his *Book of Dreams*, he dates the Shrouded Traveler's first appearance to 1945 and notes, after a recurrence, "These 2 dreams are madness & death." In the dream, which Sal recounts in *On the Road*, he is being chased across the desert by a strange Arabian figure who finally catches him just before he can reach the Protective City. Sal's first thought is that the figure is himself, wearing a shroud, but this explanation does not satisfy him. "Something, some spirit was pursuing all of us across the desert of life and was bound to catch us before we reached heaven," he says. "Naturally, now that I look back on it, this is only death: death will overtake us before heaven."

But then he turns and associates the figure with birth: "The one thing that we yearn for in our living days, that makes us sigh and groan and undergo sweet nauseas of all kinds, is the remembrance of some lost bliss that was probably experienced in the womb and can only be reproduced (though we hate to admit it) in death. But who wants to die? In the rush of events I kept thinking about this in the back of my mind. I told it to Dean and he instantly recognized it as the mere simple longing for pure death; and because we're all of us never in life again, he, rightly, would have nothing to do with it, and I agreed with him then."

Kerouac explored the Shrouded Traveler image further in his letters and journals, and eventually returned to it in *On the Road*, in Sal's apocalyptic vision of Dean rampaging across the desert toward him, "pursuing me like the Shrouded Traveler on the plain, bearing down on me." The hooded figure, he wrote in December 1948, "is ever-present and ever-pursuing. . . . The thing is central to our existence, and alone is our everlasting companion after parents and wives and children and friends may fade away. Wolfe's 'brother Loneliness,' Melville's 'inscrutable thing,' Blake's 'gate of Wrath,' Emily Dickinson's 'third event,' Shakespeare's 'nature'?—God? . . . What's left after everything else has collapsed. It's really one's 'Fate.'"

Melville's "inscrutable thing," to take one of these, appears in a remarkable speech by Captain Ahab on the nature of reality. After Starbuck, the chief mate, chides him that the white whale is just a dumb beast acting on instinct, Ahab warns him not to trust his senses, which don't see the metaphysical world lying behind this one. "All visible objects, man, are but as pasteboard masks," Ahab says. "But in each event—in the living act, the undoubted deed—there, some unknown but still reasoning thing puts forth the mouldings of its features from behind the unreasoning mask. If man will strike, strike through the mask! How can the prisoner reach outside except by thrusting through the wall? To me, the white whale is that wall, shoved near to me. Sometimes I think there's naught beyond. But 'tis enough. He tasks me; he heaps me; I see in him outrageous strength, with an inscrutable malice sinewing it. That inscrutable thing is chiefly what I hate; and be the white whale agent, or be the white whale principal, I will wreak that hate upon him. Talk not to me of blasphemy, man; I'd strike the sun if it insulted me."

This speech is madness, especially in the last line, but it gets to what Sal is looking for in his travels: *knowing time* in a way that includes the world behind our own, in which the Shrouded Traveler's two meanings—the womb and the tomb—are parts of a continuous loop. The hidden other world, though inscrutable, holds the reasons behind the unreasoning mask; it is the narrative behind the narrative. It resembles nothing so much as the storyteller's factory.

Kerouac was still puzzling over the riddle of the Shrouded Traveler in spring 1949, with no resolution in sight. He told Ed White that the dream proved to him "that there is definitely another world . . . the world which appears to us from out of our own shrouded existence which was given in darkness, before the light of life arrived. But though we're born in darkness of the womb (of time etc.) it is true that we die in light. . . . What is the Shrouded Dream after all? It is perhaps the vision of hell from which we came, and from which we tend, towards heaven, here, now. It all needs further explanation, and is the most serious matter I can think of."

Life and Death at the Movies

Sal finds himself in another hellish vision of the womb toward the end of the third journey, at the all-night theater on Detroit's skid row, where he and Dean go to crash for thirty-five cents. We know right away that the theater is hallowed ground because it exudes the spirit of two holy ghosts. "Hassel had been here on Detroit Skid Row, he had dug every shooting gallery and all-night movie and every brawling bar with his dark eyes many a time," Sal says. "His ghost haunted us. We'd never find him on Times Square again. We thought maybe by accident Old Dean Moriarty was here too—but he was not."

Kerouac grew up at the movies, getting in free to theaters in Lowell because his father printed the programs. His early encounters with immaterial beings were with the images on the screen. But in Detroit, the movies are as impoverished as the zombie clientele. "The picture was Singing Cowboy Eddie Dean and his gallant white horse Bloop, that was number one; number two double-feature film was George Raft, Sidney Greenstreet, and Peter Lorre in a picture about Istanbul." (This is Raoul Walsh's formulaic 1943 *Background to Danger*.) The two movies are a travesty of travel myths; after so many miles, Sal and Dean are trapped inside the worst of Hollywood's imaginary landscapes.

Like Sal's dream of the Shrouded Traveler, the double feature provides a cyclical model of time, interchanging beginnings and ends. "We saw both of these things six times each during the night," Sal says. "We saw them waking, we heard them sleeping, we sensed them dreaming, we were permeated completely with the strange Gray Myth of the West and the weird dark Myth of the East when morning came. All my actions since then have been dictated automatically to my subconscious by this horrible osmotic experience." These images are part of the landscape for Sal's and Dean's travels, no less than the Mississippi or the Rockies. They are insubstantial but inescapable, a kind of ghost that can move in space but not time.

As the movies penetrate Sal's sleep, he imagines himself riding them back into a deathlike womb. This is the only scene in which Sal is watched—he calls on Dean to tell him what happened.

> I was sleeping with my head on the wooden arm of a seat as six attendants of the theater converged with their night's total of swept-up rubbish and created a huge dusty pile that reached to my nose as I snored head down—till they almost swept me away too. This was reported to me by Dean, who was watching from ten seats behind. All the cigarette butts, the bottles, the matchbooks, the come and the gone were swept up in this pile. Had they taken me with it, Dean would never have seen me again. He would have had to roam the entire United States and look in every garbage pail from coast to coast before he found me embryonically convoluted among the rubbishes of my life, his life, and the life of everybody concerned and not concerned. What would I have said to him from my rubbish womb? "Don't bother me, man, I'm happy where I am. You lost me one night in Detroit in August nineteen forty-nine. What right have you to come and disturb my reverie in this pukish can?"

It is one of Sal's few glimpses of contentment, however sordid, but it is gone as quickly as it arrived. Like Faust, Sal cannot stop for contentment.

The novel does not explain why the guys are in Detroit, but in the scroll draft they go there to see Edie Parker, Kerouac's first wife, with hopes of patching up their marriage. It is a fool's errand, and when they see Edie slipping off with her new boyfriend, Neal has to explain the obvious to Jack. (Remember, Kerouac used everybody's real names in the scroll.)

After losing this illusion, Kerouac muses on his dual relationship with Neal, who is both his friend and a character in his story. He and Cassady, he decides, are like Louis-Ferdinand Céline and the ambiguous character Leon Robinson from *Journey to the End of the Night*, a book that influenced Kerouac greatly. In Céline's semiautobiographical novel the narrator admires Robinson as an embodiment of all his own worst qualities, unchecked by moral restraints or timidity. "I had definitely learned a thing or two by following Robinson in the night," the narrator, Ferdinand, says, sounding like Sal on Dean. Like many readers, Kerouac suspected that Robinson is not meant to be a real person but a projection of the narrator, able to journey *all the way* to the end of the night in a way that the narrator can't, because he has to live to tell the story.

This scene is as close as Kerouac came to explaining his relationship to his characters. Doesn't Neal, the character, perform the same function for him—getting Jack onto the road and then destroying himself on it, leaving Jack to tell the tale? "Already in New York when I couldn't sleep," Céline writes, "I racked my brains wondering if it mightn't be possible to go further and still further with Robinson." Aren't Neal's desires really unchecked projections of Jack's? "Neal was like myself," Kerouac writes in the scene, "for I'd had a dream of Neal the night before in the hotel, and Neal was me."

In the scroll draft, this meditation sets up the scene in the all-night theater. Malcolm Cowley considered the visit to Edie extraneous, so this setup is lost. The image that follows the theater scene is the book's most Céline-like, sending Sal back to a womb even darker, from 1942. "I was the star in one of the filthiest dramas of all time," he says. "I was a seaman, and went to the Imperial Café on Scollay Square in Boston to drink; I drank sixty glasses of beer and retired to the toilet bowl and went to sleep. During the night at least a hundred seamen and assorted civilians came in and cast their sentient debouchements on me till I was unrecognizably caked.* What difference does it make after all?—anonymity in the world of men is better than fame in heaven, for what's heaven? what's earth? All in the mind."

All these incorporeal figures—ghosts, spirits, memories and movie images—educate Sal in the world beyond his own. Dean can prod him on his way, but like Céline's Robinson, Dean cannot get there himself. For Dean the other world holds only an ending, not a womb. His reaction to the Shrouded Traveler is to run away, not to ponder the nature of death. "He didn't believe in a good God," Carolyn Cassady said after Neal's death. "He demanded proof, and to him the proof would be if God were stronger than his own will and his own desires. God could stop him, and then he would believe in him."

Even for Sal, the succession of womb images does not complete his education. "All I wanted," Kerouac says in the scroll draft, "and all Neal wanted and all anybody wanted was some kind of penetration into the heart of things where, like in a womb, we could curl up and sleep the ecstatic sleep that Burroughs was experiencing with a good big mainline shot of M. and advertising executives were experiencing with twelve Scotch & Sodas in

---

* In the scroll draft these are piss and puke—no telling why Kerouac got all arty about it.

Stouffers before they made the drunkard's train to Westchester—but without the hangovers." The movie images are instructive but trashy; they are not the pearl he has been promised. The strange Gray Myth of the West and the weird dark Myth of the East are poor substitutes for the revelations of travel. Singing Cowboy Eddie Dean and his horse Bloop are, at best, sights along the road, reminding him to look for revelation behind the pasteboard mask. He is still trying to learn his prophecy. When he is ready, the skies open to him in divine revelation, leading him away from Dean.

When I say I want to burn and I want to feel and I want to bridge from this life to the others, that is what I meant:—to go to the other world, or that is, keep in contact with it till I get there. . . . I must be in contact with as much of this world (through means of variety of sensuality, i.e., experience loves of all kinds).

—Journal, August 1949

SAL'S visions organize the book, giving each journey a theme and purpose, and providing an arc for the novel. They lead him from a scary image of himself to a cuddly recognition of the almighty Pooh Bear. Like the book itself, the visions begin with loss and end with God.

On the first trip, Sal's out-of-body experience in Des Moines unsubtly marks the beginning of his travels. Here, at the dividing line between the East of his youth and the West of his future, the vision shows Sal the self he is leaving behind, ghostlike because it hasn't really lived. On this trip, Sal also has his first premonition of a character Kerouac called the Great Walking Saint. This recurring figure, a central casting "old man with white hair," is Sal's prophecy coach, helping him learn to tell a story. He enters the novel first as a feeling Sal has in Colorado that somewhere across the night, the old man "was probably walking toward us with the Word, and would arrive any minute and make us silent."

The Saint makes three appearances in *On the Road*, silent until the last and sketchy even then. Kerouac described him in greater detail in a 1950 letter to Holmes from Mexico, written after Cassady left him to get on with his wives and his woes. (Instead of slogging right home, as Sal does in the novel, Kerouac stayed on in Mexico City with Burroughs, where he smoked a lot of pot, read the Bible and worked simultaneously on *On the Road* and *Doctor Sax*.) Unsettled by his first bullfight, Kerouac had a vision of a Great Walking Saint, "who, as a penance, walks around America till the day of his death. . . . He sits in the middle of Mexican shacktowns in the afternoon and chatters with the people in his own strange tongue they can all understand. He walks on. He will do so till he's a hundred years old. I decided to do this from seventy on . . . or sixty on . . . or anytime. Meanwhile it goes in my book. Someday like old Gogol and old Tolstoy, why not, I will do that . . . if it comes to pass that the light is not of this world. I have seen the light. That's what is at the end of the night. The Light. That Which God Hath Wrought. The Light." The Saint belongs to a line of writers, including the great Russians, and his travels are a penance for the sins of the world. This is the role that Sal hopes to assume over the course of the novel. For now, though, the Saint keeps his distance.

Sal gets a glimpse of the promised Light at the end of the second journey, after Dean abandons him in San Francisco, shattering his faith. With holy Dean out of the picture, Sal sets about establishing his own credentials as a seer, telling Marylou his dreams. (In the scroll draft, she holds him by the cock at the time, but this was lost in the editing.) "I told her about the big snake of the world that was coiled in the earth like a worm in an apple," he says. The snake is Satan, he explains. "A saint called Doctor Sax will destroy it with secret herbs which he is at this very moment cooking up in his underground shack somewhere in America. It may also be disclosed that the snake is just a husk of doves; when the snake dies great clouds of seminal-gray doves will flutter out and bring tidings of peace around the world."

The dream became part of *Doctor Sax*, Kerouac's fantasia of childhood memories, dreams, bedtime stories, comic books and other bits of uncorrupted consciousness. Cassady thought this inward digging was more promising than *On the Road* and that Kerouac should merge the two novels in one massive work. Kerouac could have written the scene in the hotel room with Marylou as hot and sexy, with Sal finally getting his flesh on the blonde, but instead he makes Sal a visionary child, open to whatever might be revealed to him next. His travels haven't aged him; in his weariness, he's regained some of the vision that adulthood dulls.

Sal's vision at the fish and chips joint follows immediately. Though Kerouac's private writings refer repeatedly to Jesus and the scriptures, he describes Sal's first encounter with God in language more trippy than biblical: "the potent and inconceivable radiancies shining in bright Mind Essence, innumerable lotus-lands falling open in the magic mothswarm of heaven." Instead of drawing on the language and imagery of his Catholic education, Kerouac presents Sal's personal discovery as a freestanding truth.

The prose falters in this no-man's-land. The shadows are "timeless," the radiancies are "inconceivable," the roar is "indescribable." With revelations like this, who needs blindness?

The description unwinds in diminishing similes, as if the material world were forcing its way back into Sal's consciousness. "I felt sweet, swinging bliss, like a big shot of heroin in the mainline vein," he writes; "like a gulp of wine late in the afternoon and it makes you shudder; my feet tingled. I thought I was going to die the very next moment. But I didn't die, and walked four miles and picked up ten long butts and took them back to Marylou's hotel room and poured their tobacco in my old pipe and lit up." In three sentences, his measure of the divine has shrunk from a shot of heroin to a tingle in his feet to a hit of tobacco.

The vision ends with a prosaic echo of the *Doctor Sax* dream, now reduced to "white doves in a Chinese grocery window." Instead of bringing "tidings of peace around world," as in the dream, the birds are now just groceries. The vision of the other world is gone—and with it Sal's childlike state. Sal comes away from the experience not enlightened but broken. "That was the way Dean found me when he finally decided I was worth saving," he says. The vision's vagueness gives him nothing to hang on to. Kerouac has met his challenge and recoiled.

By the third journey, as Sal gives up his identity in the lilac night, he also loses interest in his celestial visions. Now he is willing to name the God he sees, but not to pay much attention. "As we crossed the Colorado-Utah border," he says, "I saw God in the sky in the form of huge gold sunburning clouds above the desert that seemed to point a finger at me and say, 'Pass here and go on, you're on the road to heaven.' Ah well, alackaday, I was more interested in some old rotted covered wagons and pool tables sitting in the Nevada desert near a Coca-Cola stand."

Alackaday? In fact he is on the road to Salt Lake City, Dean's birthplace, with a couple of pimps. God's only message is to keep moving, like Eden's other exiles. On this journey, in which Dean becomes the Holy Goof, with "tremendous revelations . . . pouring into him all the time now," revelation itself has lost its value. Sal's vision of God can't match the osmotic impact of the double feature on Detroit's skid row. The journey ends with Sal introducing Dean to wife number three, Inez, in a meeting generated not by God but by the movies. "I was drunk and told her he was a cowboy," Sal says. "Oh, I've always wanted to meet a cowboy," she replies, and within a paragraph she gives birth to Dean's fourth child. No wonder God tells Sal to remain on the move. And no wonder readers have blown past the Christian underpinnings: Even Sal is sometimes more interested in desert junk.

Streams of Gold

The visions build toward the fourth trip, when Sal finally meets the Walking Saint and gets his prophecy. As Sal edges away from Dean on this trip, the Walking Saint comes closer. Sal spies a figure in the Colorado cliffs, "someone walking, walking, but we could not see; maybe that old man with the white hair I had sensed years ago up in the peaks. Zacatecan Jack. But he was coming closer to me, if only ever just behind."

The visions in Mexico are some of the book's richest writing, moving from hallucinatory images to biblical ones. After all their deprivations, Sal and Dean now land in a paradise of enormous spliffs, young hookers and pesos that go forever. "We've finally got to heaven," Dean says. The skies open up in a psychedelic light show. Stoned out of his mind, Sal feels as if he is "recoiling from some gloriously riddled glittering treasure-box that you're afraid to look at because of your eyes, they bend inward, the riches and the treasures are too much to take all at once. I gulped. I saw streams of gold pouring through the sky and right across the tattered roof of the poor old car, right across my eyeballs and indeed right inside them; it was everywhere. . . . For a long time I lost consciousness in my lower mind of what we were doing and only came around sometime later when I looked up from fire and silence like waking from sleep to the world, or waking from void to a dream."

All they get for this vision, though, is the frenzy of the whore-house, which Sal concedes is "a pornographic hasheesh daydream in heaven." The mambo, girls and weed are pleasant enough, but they don't provide the guys any larger purpose in which to lose themselves for good. In the Mexican dark, Sal sees "an appari-tion" reminiscent of *Moby-Dick*'s white whale: "a wild horse, white as a ghost, came trotting down the road directly toward Dean. . . . the horse was white as snow and immense and almost phosphorescent and easy to see." In Melville's novel, the white beast shatters the *Pequod*, but Sal's phantom horse simply trots past the car "like a ship." Sal has reached a gentler world than Melville's; he's discovered a pacific spirit behind the pasteboard mask, where Ahab found only his own destruction.

But as the Mexican visions become more biblical, with Sal rousing Dean to "wake up and see the shepherds, wake up and see the golden world that Jesus came from," they raise apocalyp-tic implications that Kerouac doesn't explore. Watching the idealized peasants on a premodern landscape, Sal notes that someday the bomb will bring his country to a similar state. "[A]nd they never dreamed the sadness and broken delusion of it," he says: that through nuclear self-destruction his world might become as poor and Edenic as theirs. In Sal's cyclical con-ception of time, the primitive landscape represents America's future as well as its past—both states preferable to the present.

Kerouac touched on this millenarian mind-set in his 1957 essay "About the Beat Generation," professing his peers' desire "to be gone, out of this world (which is not our kingdom), 'high,' ecstatic, saved, as if the visions of the cloistral saints of Chartres and Clairvaux were back with us again bursting like weeds through the sidewalks of stiffened Civilization wearying through its late motions." In *On the Road*, Sal stops short of hastening poor Civ's trip through these final gestures. But his prescription for revelation is collapse—for individuals by breaking down the rational mind and for civilizations by more cataclysmic scenarios.

The Shocking Passage

"When daybreak came we were zooming through New Jersey with the great cloud of Metropolitan New York rising before us in the snowy distance. Dean had a sweater wrapped around his ears to keep warm. He said we were a band of Arabs coming to blow up New York."

Reading this passage now takes your breath away. It's pure coincidence, certainly, but intriguing for *On the Road*'s parallel with another road book: the Egyptian writer Sayyid Qutb's *Milestones*, based on his travels in America during the same years, which became the central text of the Islamist jihad movement— its *Mein Kampf*, as Jonathan Raban calls it. Qutb was attending decadent church dances in Greeley, Colorado, when the gang was spinning Dizzy Gillespie records in Denver. Like Kerouac, Qutb saw America as a materialistic society corrupted by modernism, in need of spiritual awakening. His book, too, is an inspiration to young men today. And like Kerouac, he suffered backlash from the critics: Gamal Abdel Nasser had him hanged in 1966.

Since Sal doesn't believe in collective reform, he seems to accept nuclear holocaust as an inevitable relief from postwar America. As Dean said earlier, watching a boy toss rocks at cars, "God exists without qualms." When the Old Saint finally gives Sal his prophecy on his way back north, it is an acknowledgement of human suffering, not a cure: "Go moan for man."

It's the End of the World as We Know It (and I Feel Fine)

The mystery of these visions isn't what Sal sees but what he (and we) take away from them. Sal often seems to have little inner life, passively moving with whatever comes his way. When God appears to him in revelation, his reaction is to stare dumbstruck until the vision passes, then go along with whatever happens next. He's eager to explore the world but unwilling to synthesize his observations, lest he diminish or distort them. This leaves his visions aloof and disconnected, fragments in a fragmentary road journal.

The visions do the work of the narrator's inner life: Since he won't stop to think about what he's doing, they stop the action for him. They turn the book outward, away from psychology and the individual, toward God and the universal. Kerouac intended *On the Road* not as a private journal but a broad account of "what I mean and what I think we all mean." He dismissed his friends' obsession with their shrinks, which he felt whittled the world down to private neuroses, just as unhappiness diminished Tolstoy's unhappy families to their own secular idiosyncrasies. "And what a revelation to know that I was born sad," Kerouac wrote in his journals—"that it was no trauma that made me so sad—but God:—who made me that way."

So what are we supposed to do with the visions? Instead of driving the narrative, they bring it to a standstill. No amount of herb will compel American college students to stay up all night trying to unpack them. They're the most emphatic part of Sal's story and the least reliable, always brought on by fatigue, drugs, hunger or the blur of velocity. As a reader, you can't question or argue with the visions. If you don't accept them as divine revelation, all you can do is wait for the guys to get moving again. Sal plays the gnostic's paradox, which may be good for the spirit but is tough on the narrative: that life has a higher meaning but it is unknowable, so it appears meaningless. It took Kerouac until *Big Sur*, which moves toward a climactic vision of the cross, to deliver a vision with content equal to his language.

Sal's brushes with the divine are also self-serving, mainly justifying his own habits. Since no one can earn true knowledge the best course is to observe passively, like Sal, waiting for revelation, the more bleary-eyed the better. Until the Saint tells Sal to moan for man, the visions make no demands. This is good news for Sal, making the narrator the book's spiritual role model and his narration its heroic act. To reduce the visions to his own powers of insight would be an act of ego, but to exchange an inner life for divine vision is an expression of piety.

Revival

Kerouac's religious talk has rarely been taken seriously in secular literary circles, except as evidence of his inner turmoil and guilt. This is partly because he recoils from really delivering the visions and partly because he didn't seem to live by them. After all, he was a lush and often a lout, a bad husband and a worse father, incapable of Christian discipline, self-denial and sacrifice. His sanctimony has seemed a defense mechanism against criticism or a substitute for honest soul-searching. It's easier to genuflect than to tackle one's sexuality or mommy complex. Also, to many readers, Kerouac's God stuff is just uncool.

To a great extent, the visions have survived without their

Christian connotations, seen as part of the Beats' debt to William Blake or, more broadly, their interest in drugs. Ginsberg famously hallucinated the spirit of Blake speaking to him in 1948, after a session of reading and masturbation. The Beats' pre-hippie consciousness, he said later, "was a visionary experience in 1948," but now "everybody sees and understands these things."

The sixties counterculture provided a liberal gloss for Kerouac's religiosity, without such off-putting considerations as suffering, penance or Jesus. Watching the younger people at Kerouac's funeral in 1969, Holmes realized that they had built Jack's lonely visionary impulses into a collective lifestyle. "They were forming communes, and the spiritual perspectives, the religious ecstasies of which he had written were the common coinage of these endeavors. Visionary drugs, music as group sacrament, the nonviolent witness to the holiness of all sentient life—all this had surfaced as he knew it would, and, far from being derided in the media or patronized by the Academy (as had happened in this case), it was being heralded as the unique culture of a New Age." What they took up was his license to handcraft his own belief system, not the beliefs he chose. Because Kerouac always clams up at the moment of revelation, it's been easy to embrace his visions strictly for the pretty colors. As the man said, alackaday.

But Kerouac's mysticism also parallels a more conservative Christian movement that began at the time of his travels and has proved as powerful and lasting as the Woodstock nation. Billy Graham, who was four years older than Kerouac, held his first crusade in 1947 and came to national prominence in 1949 with an eight-week tent revival in Los Angeles. Graham, too, incited an ecstatic youth movement dissatisfied with the materialism of secular society. Like Kerouac, Graham stressed earthshaking individual conversion experiences rather than intellectual engagement or study. "Billy Graham is very hip," Kerouac told an interviewer. "What's Graham say, 'I'm going to turn out spiritual babies'? That's Beatness. But he doesn't know it. The Beat Generation has no interest in politics, only mysticism, that's their religion. It's kids standing on the street and talking about the end of the world."

By 1965, these kids were in Costa Mesa, California, where an evangelical minister named Chuck Smith at a tiny church called Calvary Chapel reached out to the hippies and drug users who were too dirty or weird looking for other churches. It became the freak church, a collective of holy fools. Within a few years, Smith's "Jesus freaks" or "Jesus people" had outgrown a succession of buildings and were holding mass baptisms in the Pacific. They were a Protestant movement with monastic tendencies and folk guitars, whereas Kerouac was a Catholic Buddhist on a bop bender, but these differences hid more fundamental similarities. Like Kerouac, the Jesus people believed in a personal, untidy hotwire to revelation. The churches that have thrived in Calvary's wake, swelling now with suburban baby boomers and their families, call their congregants "seekers" and their faith a "walk" or "journey," which would have suited the characters of On the Road. "What's your road, man?" Dean asks Sal—"holyboy road, madman road, rainbow road, guppy road, any road. It's an anywhere road for anybody anyhow. Where body how?"

So maybe Kerouac's legacy is not Woodstock and Dockers but Costa Mesa and Christian rock. It's a thriving legacy. Though the freak image is gone, the little church in Costa Mesa now draws thirty thousand worshippers a week and has spawned nearly seven hundred Calvary Chapels worldwide, plus a splinter denomination, the Vineyard, with another six hundred churches. Seeker-sensitive churches fill giant warehouses and former shopping malls across the country. The post-Kerouac goatee now signals not Dobie Gillis but Rick Warren, the enormously popular pastor and author of *The Purpose Driven Life*.

This legacy suggests a compelling way to read Kerouac's book. The conservative Christian magazine *Touchstone* lamented recently that the book has done great harm, inspiring "countless young men to make excess and self-fulfillment their cardinal virtues and thus to remain mired in their immaturity." But the author, Stephen H. Webb, attributes this to a mass misreading of the book: "His road was not, contrary to sixties interpretations, the fast lane of immediate gratification and mindless pleasure. Instead, it was the ultimate test of both physical and spiritual endurance. . . . Sal's goal in *On the Road* is not to discover himself but to lose himself to something greater. The whole point of being on the road was to seek the metaphysical roots of human suffering. He wants to find in America a strange new world that defies the materialism and conformity of the fifties." Kerouac would likely have agreed with this reading, even as he rejected more popular celebratory ones. It makes *On the Road* a powerful and singularly gloomy book, but good.

Sal's final vision is not a vision at all, but an understanding of God's nature. Sal finishes his journeys without his father, Dean, Old Dean or the stimuli of travel. Sitting on a Hudson pier, he muses, "and tonight the stars'll be out, and don't you know that God is Pooh Bear?" He's returned to childlike vision, at great personal cost but also gain. God is a mystery—but a playful one, not a wrathful one. And life for the saved is a Hundred Acre Wood.

Kerouac saw the secular counterculture as a tragic misinterpretation of his intentions. Among the freaks of Costa Mesa he might have found a home, at least for a while, until he ran off again—a ghost, a visionary, a dharma bum, a holy fool looking for his Pooh Bear. Even the freaks never caught up with that one.

The Aftermath

Sad Paradise and the Lessons Unlearned

If you don't think I did all that stuff, look at me.

—Remark to Richard Hill, 1969

[T]he person who creates a new society will have no place in that society himself.

—Gregory Corso on Kerouac

KEROUAC named his narrator after misreading a line in a 1947 Ginsberg poem. "Sad paradise it is I imitate / And fallen angels whose wings are sighs." The sadness in Ginsberg's line proved prophetic. After writing his scroll draft, Kerouac spent the next six years producing manuscripts that no publisher wanted, shuttling between temporary homes with no money or professional recognition, his marriage ruined and his former athletic vigor mocked by phlebitis in his legs. On one trip, he was reduced to eating grass. "What have I got?" he wrote to Holmes in 1952. "I'm 30 years old, broke, my wife hates me and is trying to have me jailed, I have a daughter I'll never see, my mother after all this time and work and worry and hopes is STILL working her ass off in a shoe shop; I have not a cent in my pocket for a decent whore." His wings, truly, were sighs.

He had no way of knowing that success would be worse.

He never benefited from the lessons of Sal Paradise. The stable family life that Sal plotted out eluded Kerouac. Sal's visions brought Kerouac no buffer for his daily struggles. As Kerouac got older, the gap between *On the Road*'s ideals of manhood and the life he led only widened. Like Sal, he was ambitious in his dreams but passive in his follow-through. Both looked for redemption to come from the outside, like lightning in a clear blue sky. In the end, Kerouac was as remote from Sal as Sal was from his mad ones, a passive observer of the swirl he helped create.

In the time it took *On the Road* to reach print, the nature of public life changed in ways for which Kerouac was constitutionally unsuited. The television set, a novelty when he started his travels, had infiltrated seven million homes by 1957, expanding the reach and demands of celebrity. Elvis Presley, Marlon Brando and James Dean had galvanized the public around a particular image of sexy, brooding, inarticulate youth. While Kerouac's manuscript languished, the country experienced fast food, *Playboy*, hot rods, Alan Freed, *Brown* v. *Board of Education*, the Marlboro Man and an economic explosion entirely at odds with the book's skid row mysticism. "Never has a whole people spent so much money on so many expensive things in such an easy way as Americans are doing today," crowed *Fortune* magazine in 1956. The book's bop saints had become the public face of heroin addiction; Charlie Parker died on Kerouac's birthday.

For a shy, good-looking, confused writer, the spotlight of 1957 was brighter, harsher and more cannibalistic than anything he could have imagined when he started the book nine years earlier. It liked controversy and lifestyle voyeurism more than literary or spiritual aspiration. His book launched him into media that weren't his, and he couldn't survive the trip.

All of that was unknowable in 1951. When Kerouac finished the scroll draft, he spent a month revising and retyping it before showing it to Robert Giroux at Harcourt Brace. His marriage to Joan Haverty was over, an ending he chose not to include in *On the Road*. He pronounced the novel "a great book, my very best, one of the best to be published this year anywhere," but as he awaited Giroux's verdict, he wrote to Cassady with a mix of self-pity and adolescent fantasy: "Now I'm in Lucien's loft—alone—cold rainy afternoon—tossed & pitched all night long—Ah shit man I think I'll just go to Mexcity and build me a topflight pad & relax in coolness, kicks, food, mistresses, main once-a-week etc. heh? Get me an LP record player & great LP Charlie Christian album—Burroughs leaving Mexcity he says—I will dig Mex on lush this time and explore great Mexico. How awful it would be if I hadn't writ this On the Road!"

Two weeks later, these fantasies crashed when Giroux did not buy the manuscript. The two men gave different accounts of how the non-deal went down, but in any case, the experience devastated Kerouac. He had upheld his part of the manly bargain, and now he was denied his due. "[T]hey don't even read Dosty and don't care about all that shit and bums etc.," he told Cassady. "Because of this, Allen re-reads my book and decides it is really beat after all. Lucien thinks it's shit. John Holmes still stands by it. I know you would like it. Anyway here I go. Don't know what to do. Have no money to even GO to your attic; and once there, would have to work; and have necessity of writing further book in peace & silence. Nothing to do."

By October 1951, he had started yet another draft of *On the Road*, first as a series of inserts to the scroll manuscript, then as an entirely new version. The new book covered much of the same ground but added transcripts of stoned conversations with Cassady and stream-of-consciousness passages written using the spontaneous method he modeled after Ed White's rapid architectural sketches. Parts read like jazz improvisations on the chords of *On the Road*. This was the voice he'd been looking for all along—or so it seemed at the time. It transformed the novel "from conventional narrative survey of road trips etc. into a big multi-dimensional conscious and subconscious character invocation of Neal in his whirlwinds," he wrote. He now disparaged the scroll voice as an imitation of Burroughs channeling Dashiell Hammett. He pronounced the new book a masterpiece. "It is like *Ulysses* and should be treated as such," he told Ginsberg.

Mistakes, He Made a Few

When Kerouac changed his characters' names or identities after the scroll draft, he left a few stones unturned. In New Orleans, Old Bull Lee reverts briefly to his real name, Bill, for a night on the town: "Dean and I were yelling about a big night in New Orleans and wanted Bill to show us around. He threw a damper on this." And Kerouac's sister, who became Sal's brother Rocco, regained her gender when police stop Sal, Dean and Sal's aunt carrying furniture north in the Hudson. "[T]his furniture isn't stolen; it's my niece's," the aunt says—but really it's her nephew's.

A few other anomalies have defied the years and copy editors. On the third trip to Denver, after the argument in the urinal, Sal teases readers, "All kinds of tremendous complications arose that night when Dean and I went to stay with the Okie family"; but a few pages later the complications remain abed: "Nothing happened that night; we went to sleep."

Gabrielle's transformation into Sal's aunt also left a more philosophical hole: As Sal moans for his and Dean's lost fathers, the book says nothing about his lost *mother*, except perhaps to recycle her as a fish fryer whom Sal calls "my strange Dickensian mother" from a past life, frowning on her "sullen, unloved, mean-minded son."

Tim Hunt, among others, has argued that this 1952 novel, which was finally published in 1973 as *Visions of Cody*, is really the final draft of *On the Road*, and that the version that made Kerouac famous was just one of four preliminary drafts. Kerouac opened the door to this assessment by calling the new book *On the Road* (he considered subtitling it *A Modern Novel*, as a nod to modern jazz), and later referring to the previous work as "the 20-day 'On the Road,'" as if it were an exercise rather than a finished novel. Even *Visions* wasn't the last word. In October 1952, he told friends he was starting yet another *On the Road*, this one a thousand-page epic, and that he would retitle the previous one *Visions of N.P.*

It's hard to know Kerouac's attitude toward his manuscripts, especially as the rejections piled up. He kept fastidious files of all his correspondence, but carelessly mailed his only copies of manuscripts to friends who might be halfway around the world. If publishers and critics had immediately fallen for the scroll *Road*, would he have shared their satisfaction and written more in the same vein? Or would he have continued to change styles and forms, as he continued to uproot his domestic life? When a reporter asked him how he was able to finish so many novels, since he never finished anything else, he gave a jazzman's answer. "I don't finish," he said. "I just write it continuously. Sooner or later you reach the point in a book where you feel everybody's bored, and you bring it around somehow and end it. That's deep form." *On the Road* and *Visions of Cody* might be seen as different performances of the same tune, each capturing a different night and a different high.

Ginsberg, who was acting as agent for his friends, was less impressed with the experimental version of *On the Road*. He felt Kerouac had turned rejection into martyrdom, creating a novel that put off readers before they could reject it. He told Kerouac it was unpublishable and self-indulgent, "crazy in a bad way," and "juss crappin around thoughtlessly with that trickstyle *often*, and it's not so good." To Cassady he called it "a holy mess—it's great allright but he did everything he could to fuck it up with a lot of meaningless bullshit I think, page after page of surrealist free association that don't make sense to anybody except someone who has blown Jack. . . . Jack knows that too, I'll bet—why is he tempting rejection and fate?"

Kerouac received this criticism with characteristic grace. "And you who I thought was my friend," he wrote back to Ginsberg. "Do you think I don't realize how jealous you are and how you and Holmes and [Carl] Solomon all would give your right arm to be able to write like the writing in On the Road . . . And leaving me no alternative but to write stupid letters like this when if instead you were men I could at least get the satisfaction of belting you all on the kisser—too many glasses to take off. Why you goddamn cheap little shits are all the same and always were and why did I ever listen and fawn and fart with you—15 years of my life wasted among the cruds of New York. . . . And the smell of [Holmes's] work is the smell of death . . . Everybody knows he has no talent . . . His book stinks, and your book is only mediocre, and you all know it, and my book is great and will never be published. Beware of meeting me on the street in New York."

This was another thing about Kerouac, which made colossi of his detractors and martyrdom of his life: He lived for his grievance. Even as a high school athlete he complained to the sportswriter at the Lowell Courier-Citizen when he thought he wasn't getting enough ink. He took all criticism personally, even as he courted it. In success he griped, "I'm the only major writer in America today who never won a prize. Never." He saw himself as a literary outcast, and nothing proclaimed his victimhood like the defiantly private text of the new Road.

Writers owe their fates to outside circumstances, and Kerouac's friendship with Ginsberg, which survived his best efforts to sabotage it, played a felicitous role in his career. Allen stood by him both personally and professionally through all the years of insults. (Also, as someone who had blown Jack, he was perhaps in a unique position to render judgments.) If Kerouac intended the new, experimental *On the Road* to supersede the old, Ginsberg and Holmes continued to push the more accessible version on publishers. Thus Kerouac arrived as the dashing nomad of *On the Road*, not as the overreaching Joycean of *Visions of Cody*. Ginsberg ultimately warmed to the latter book, and wrote a glowing essay to accompany its publication. More than anyone, he tirelessly promoted the Beats as a literary movement and stamped an identity on what was really a disparate group of writers.

A Man Exposed

Leslie Fiedler, who was mostly dismissive of the Beats, believed that Ginsberg "invented the legend of Jack Kerouac, this time with the collaboration of certain photographers from *Life* and the ladies' magazines, transforming the ex-Columbia University athlete, the author of a dull and conventional *Bildungsroman* remembered by no one [*The Town and the City*], into a fantasy figure capable of moving the imagination of rebellious kids with educations and literary aspirations. . . . The legend of Kerouac is, to be sure, much more interesting than any of his books, since it is the work of a more talented writer; but the young confuse the two, as, I presume, do Ginsberg and even Kerouac." In truth, the Kerouac bandwagon began with a review by Gilbert Millstein in *The New York Times*, but Fiedler was right that Kerouac was more fantasy figure than literary one. Most scholarship on

Kerouac has been about how he lived or how he wrote, not *what* he wrote. And most pop writing has focused on his contribution to the counterculture he rued. Any claims for the book's cultural impact and historical importance have relied little on its literary virtues.

Its impact on Kerouac and Cassady certainly had nothing to do with lit stuff. Seven months after publication, Cassady was arrested on drug charges, possibly in part because of the notoriety of Dean Moriarty. For Kerouac, the scrutiny was more than he could handle. He was six years removed from the book's style and ten from some of the events, and the media were more interested in his current lifestyle—the drugs, the sex, the hygiene—than in either. He played the holy fool in public, showing up drunk at readings and baring himself unguardedly in interviews, becoming a sexy beast for a celebrity industry that loved sex and monsters.

It's a staple of the Kerouac myth that he was pilloried by a square, repressive press, a view that seems to have arisen more from Kerouac's sense of injury than from the actual reviews. Ginsberg called the reviews "one of the most vicious things I've ever seen" and "an attack in the media that was so vast it looks like organized psychosis." But much of the press, including the *Times*, was supportive, and many of the negative or mixed reviews, including those by Rexroth and Herbert Gold, acknowledged Kerouac's talent and his book's importance. What's undeniable is that Kerouac's thin skin was no match for either the negative reviews or the cavils among the positive. Victimhood suited his nature, even in fat times. Success, he told Sterling Lord, "is when you can't enjoy your food any more in peace."

He developed a self-destructive relationship with his readers, alternately hiding from them and accepting their invitations to go on benders. Often he was arrested or beaten up in bars, quite seriously on at least two occasions. After a beating that sent him to the hospital in April 1958, he told friends, "maybe I got brain damage, maybe once I was kind drunk, but now am brain-clogged drunk with the kindness valve clogged by injury." Between the fans and the critics, Kerouac felt he was getting it from both sides. He referred to himself mockingly as the King of the Beats, made to wear a "crown of shit." At the White Horse Tavern in Greenwich Village, which had accommodated Dylan Thomas's most famous binges, a patron scrawled the words "Kerouac Go Home" in the men's toilet.

One of the first writers to reach a national audience through television, he never mastered the concept of small talk or self-promotion. Instead, even in media outlets he considered hostile or belittling, he talked nakedly about drugs and God and faith, trusting that he'd be taken seriously. Often he was drunk and sanctimonious at the same time, fascinating for his willingness to say inappropriate and self-damaging things. On John Wingate's *Nightbeat* show, he told a national audience—getting its first look at the wild Beat figurehead—that he was "waiting for God to show his face" and that he prayed to his brother Gerard, his father, Jesus Christ, Avalokiteshvara Buddha and Our Mother in Heaven. He told Mike Wallace, then with the *New York Post*, "It's a great burden to be alive. A heavy burden, a great big heavy burden. I wish I were safe in Heaven, dead." (Imagine Jonathan Franzen saying that in *US Weekly*.)

No one was better at misjudging an audience. At a panel discussion on the topic, "Is There a Beat Generation," Kerouac began, "The question is very silly because we should be wondering tonight, *Is there a world?* . . . Because there is really no world. Sometimes I'm walking on the ground and I see right through the ground, and there is no world." He fit neatly with the new medium's doltish male characters: He was the hard-charging mystic dummy.

If this was a spokesman for a new generation—a title Kerouac mostly disavowed—his message was garbled or misguided. In his books, he could write about himself and still remain invisible; in interviews, he said too much and revealed nothing. Eventually he became a reliable parlor act, spewing toxic nonsense about hippies and the Left. You can read all of Kerouac's interviews end to end without encountering much sign of a noteworthy intellect. Like Bob Dylan, who has talked twaddle in public for four-plus decades, the real Kerouac is best encountered through the artifice of his fiction.

Through it all, he continued to write. It was the one thing he knew how to do, so he did it. It's widely assumed that all the drinking ruined his writing, but his body of work argues otherwise. His novels are hit-and-miss, but no more so in drunken times than sober, and he wrote his best, *Big Sur*, in 1961, at the bottom of his alcoholic spiral, when his self-loathing finally pushed him to write about himself, brutally.

Kerouac consistently steered his novels away from whatever expertise he might develop, giving each book the freedom to fail on its own terms. In the end, he simply wore out the public's patience and indulgence. The revolution that was coming along behind him was brighter and shinier and more fun. After *On the Road*, he couldn't write with the same everylad's immaturity again, and his relationship with adulthood, while often fascinating, was prickly and difficult. Only a masochist would embrace

Big Sur's meltdown as an invitation to adventure, and only a misanthrope would see it as an anthem of collective experience.

The writer and critic David Gates, describing his ambivalent love affair with the Beats, noted recently that their influence can be found almost everywhere today except in contemporary literature. "Among novelists," Gates wrote, "Kerouac and Burroughs may be honored as role models of American cussedness, as familiar spirits, as Promethean innovators, as visionaries who lived on enviably intimate terms with their imaginations. But relatively few people actually want to write like either of them, and few of those few will have their work taken seriously by whatever's left of the literary establishment. A 21-year-old applying to a writing program is as ill-advised to cite Jack Kerouac as an influence as O. Henry or H.P. Lovecraft."

This is half as Kerouac would have wanted. Though he craved approval from the establishment, he boasted that the Beats "transferred literature from the colleges and academies into the hands of the folk, in the same way that rock and roll young people have transferred music composition from Tin Pan Alley to the folk." The folk, however, can be limited in their interests and unforgiving in their affections. They want affirmation, not growth. Once they embraced Kerouac as a buck-wild road buddy, all they needed was for him to flatter them in their embrace. He was proof that the world had changed—that their ways had carried the day. They didn't need him to challenge those ways.

By the time *On the Road* was published, its critique of postwar hollowness was news to no one. A federal judge, rejecting obscenity charges against Ginsberg's "Howl" in 1957, approved the poem in language that just a few years previous might have been fighting words, as "an indictment of those elements of modern society destructive of the best qualities of human nature; such elements are predominantly identified as materialism, conformity, and the mechanization leading to war." When courts rail against conformity and materialism, it's hard to be the Beat contrarian insisting on hard work and family values, or subordinating the fun to biblical penance and literary experiment.

John Holmes once remarked that America sends its artists not to the garret but to the vaudeville stage, "and later wonder[s] why they gnashed their teeth." Some thrive there, like Twain, Dizzy Gillespie or Louis Armstrong. Kerouac never got comfortable or learned how to live in the spotlight. *Time* magazine, in a mocking review from 1962, joked that Kerouac might someday grow up. "Think of the books, man, a whole new series: *The Dharma Bums Grow Up*, *The Dharma Bums on Wall Street*. Who knows, maybe even *The Dharma Bums in the White House*?" It would have given Kerouac no satisfaction that these three hypothetical titles described the contents of *Time* in the seventies, eighties and nineties, respectively.

He spent his last day at home, October 20, 1969, in front of the television in St. Petersburg, in a house with a fake brick façade, amid the embers of a third marriage, to Stella Sampas, a Lowell friend he married so she'd take care of his mother. He'd been beaten and arrested in a bar the month before, and had a Kennedy half-dollar taped over his navel to keep in his hernia. By then the public had lost interest in his steady stream of books, passing him a mantle of neglect once worn by Melville, who was commemorated at his death as a "Once Popular Author." Seated in front of *The Galloping Gourmet* with notes for a future novel, he began vomiting blood. He died in the hospital on October 21 of hemorrhaging esophageal varices, after twenty-six blood infusions. He was forty-seven.

The Lessons Less Learned

So why was Kerouac never satisfied with *On the Road*? He didn't keep rewriting *The Town and the City*, which came before it, or any of the books that came after. Imagine J. D. Salinger rewriting *The Catcher in the Rye* as a stream-of-consciousness experiment, then starting again as a thousand-page epic. Part of *On the Road*'s appeal is how much it leaves unsaid or unsolved. Even at the end, Sal has everything to learn, and readers can join in the learning. Few novels—and none of Kerouac's—are as innocent and accepting of their own ignorance. Sal discovers everything in the book for the first time, as if he were reading along with us.

There are three parties that make up any reading experience: the author, the characters and the reader, whose contribution is most often overlooked. A strength of *On the Road* is the energy readers bring to it, undiminished and unchanged after fifty years. The book's holes and gray areas free readers to build the text around their own lives. Sal's passivity, ultimately, has made for active readers a fraternity of the sentences if not the highways.

The story Kerouac told through all his books was simple. He was after emotional or spiritual truths, not intellectual ones. "I'm writing this book because we're all going to die," he wrote in *Visions of Cody*—"In the loneliness of my life, my father dead, my brother dead, my mother far away, my sister and my wife far away, nothing here but my own tragic hands that were once guarded by a world, a sweet attention, that now are left to guide and disappear their own way into the common dark of all our death, sleeping in me raw bed, alone and stupid: with just this one pride and consolation: my heart broke in the general despair, and opened inwards to the Lord, I made a supplication in this dream."

When Kerouac recited this long sentence on Steve Allen's TV show, he pretended it came from *On the Road*, the book he was there to promote. These were his enduring themes: loneliness, death, abandonment, stupidity, God, penitence and a book that didn't stay still for him, any more than it has for the millions who have read it. All he could do was to keep telling his story and, because the story required it, to live his life. The book remains relevant in part because we still feel stupid in the face of death, supplicant in the face of God, embarrassed and lonely in our pride and dreams.

On the Road braves its ignorance before these absolutes, like a Wet Hitchhiker on a blind itinerary. It doesn't offer answers. Its travels don't resolve ignorance but affirm it; they don't forestall suffering but accept it as part of the human condition. What better reasons could there be for characters to hit the road, or for readers to join the journey? Life is ignorance and suffering and jazz and loss and occasional revelation. So is the road—as much at the beginning as at the end. And still we travel, and still we live, because what else can we do? And at some point we read *On the Road*, which turns this elemental recognition into a lively story, with girls, visions, everything.

The people in this book are, with a few exceptions, no longer here to tell their story. The places, highways, drugs, jazz and cars have all changed or disappeared. You could wave your thumb at the hostile traffic in Shelton, Nebraska, in 2007 and not learn anything about what it meant to Sal Paradise in 1947.

Whenever possible, I've relied on texts written during the years Kerouac was living and writing *On the Road*, principally his journals, letters and drafts of the novel itself. I take these as windows on Kerouac's mind at that moment, not the last word on facts and events—more creative performances than historical documents. Tim Hunt suggests that Kerouac's novels are a "biography of his self-image" rather than an autobiography. I think his writings, taken together, are a *novel* of his self-image, an effort to will that self-image into being. So I quote them as artifacts from a moment in time, always in need of deciphering, and true in the way that good novels are true.

Most are published and readily available. Ann Charters artfully culled two volumes of letters (New York: Viking, 1995 and 1999), and Douglas Brinkley edited selections from the journals into a single volume, *Windblown World* (New York: Viking, 2004). Kerouac's letters to Ed White were published in *The Missouri Review* in an issue titled "Living on the Fringe" (vol. 17, no. 3, 1994). In *As Ever*, Barry Gifford compiled letters between Ginsberg and Cassady (Berkeley: Creative Arts, 1977), and *Collected Letters, 1944–1967*, edited by Dave Moore, gathers much of Neal's correspondence as well as Carolyn's letters to him (New York:

Penguin, 2004). The Harry Ransom Humanities Center at the University of Texas at Austin cleared up a long-standing typo in Ginsberg's letters to Neal. Thanks to John Sampas for permission to quote from unpublished letters from Kerouac to Holmes, a transcendent body of correspondence awaiting a publisher.

Besides the scroll draft and final draft of *On the Road*, I quote from other Kerouac books: *Big Sur, Visions of Cody, The Dharma Bums, Visions of Gerard, Vanity of Duluoz, Desolation Angels, Book of Dreams, Mexico City Blues* and *Lonesome Traveler*. Also the following essays: "Beatific: The Origins of the Beat Generation," "About the Beat Generation," "Lamb, No Lion," "The Beginning of Bop," "Belief & Technique for Modern Prose," "Essentials of Spontaneous Prose" and "Is There a Beat Generation?" Except for the last, an address at Hunter College, the essays are all in *The Portable Jack Kerouac* (New York: Viking, 1995). His address there can be heard on *The Jack Kerouac Collection* (Rhino, 1990).

Paul Maher Jr.'s *Empty Phantoms* helpfully collects "Interviews and Encounters" with Kerouac—a further extension of the creative process, valuable more for the light it sheds on the speaker than for what he says (New York: Thunder's Mouth Press, 2005). I quote from interviews or articles by Richard Hill, Andrew O'Hagan, Jack McClintock, Al Aronowitz, John Clellon Holmes, Kenneth Allsop and Mike Wallace, and a Q&A press release for *Visions of Gerard*. Kerouac's *Paris Review* interview with Ted Berrigan and Aram Saroyan is online at theparisreview.com.

Kerouac biographies are a peculiar animal. He wrote about his life in such detail that the biographer's role becomes to refute the novels or repeat them. Yet scholars have taken on this task and produced good works. I leaned variously on those by Gerald Nicosia, Barry Gifford and Lawrence Lee, Dennis McNally, Charters, Barry Miles and Ellis Amburn (discussed individually below) as well as William Plummer's clip-job biography of Cassady, *The Holy Goof* (New York: Thunder's Mouth Press, 1981). All come with one major caveat: Each relies at times on the novels as factual accounts, which makes for both dubious biography and circular literary scholarship. We read the biographies for leverage on the novels, which is impossible when both flow from the same source.

Of the bios, Nicosia's *Memory Babe* (New York: Grove Press, 1983) is the most detailed and best documented. I especially relied on it for details of Kerouac's childhood; direct quotations of Tom Livornese and Kerouac on his sexual parameters and desire for an award were taken from the book with permission from Gerald Nicosia. Gifford and Lee, in *Jack's Book* (New York: St. Martin's Press, 1978), a semi-oral history, grant Kerouac's friends long quotations to describe their contradictory lives with him. It's my favorite as a read. McNally's *Desolate Angel* (New York: Random House, 1979) feels the most empathetic and does a good job with the backlash. Miles's *Jack Kerouac: King of the Beats* (London: Virgin Books, 2002) and Amburn's *Subterranean Kerouac* (New York: St. Martin's Press, 1999) both seem to begin with opinions about Kerouac (bad man, weird sexuality, respectively) and encounter little to challenge these. Miles wrote a better biography of Ginsberg, and I relied on him mainly for perspectives on Jack and Allen. Charters's *Kerouac: A Biography* (San Francisco: Straight Arrow Press, 1973) started it all in 1973. If other scholars have surpassed it, all remain in her debt. Beat scholarship has yet to produce a brilliant critic, but she has been a resourceful and tireless one.

Joyce Johnson's *Minor Characters* (New York: Houghton Mifflin, 1983) is the single best-written book on Kerouac, but it covers only a short period of his life and is most interesting on

Elise Cowen and Johnson herself. Johnson outshines Jack in their published correspondence, *Door Wide Open* (New York: Viking, 2000), but it's possible the relationship meant more to her. Holmes's *Nothing More to Declare* (New York: E. P. Dutton, 1967), *Gone in October: Last Reflections on Jack Kerouac* (Boise: Limberlost Press, 1985) and Carolyn Cassady's *Off the Road* (New York: William Morrow, 1990) provide sympathetic apologies for Jack and Neal, respectively. Holmes articulates the Beats' intentions but never accounts for their failings. As for Cassady—well, your heart goes out to her for what she put up with, but her kindness inspires more admiration than total trust. Joan Haverty Kerouac's caustic *Nobody's Wife* (Berkeley: Creative Arts, 1990) provides a valuable and frightening portrait of Kerouac's relationship with his mother.

Two anthologies I found useful are Charters's *Beat Down to Your Soul: What Was the Beat Generation?* (New York: Penguin, 2001) and *The Rolling Stone Book of the Beats*, edited by Holly George-Warren (New York: Hyperion, 1999). From the former, I quote pieces by Burroughs, Robert Stone, Norman Podhoretz, Warren Tallman and David L. Ulin. From the *Rolling Stone* book I quote from Brinkley's essay on Kerouac, which noted Jack's friendship with William F. Buckley, and Gina Berriault's interview with Carolyn Cassady, as well as pieces by Parke Puterbaugh and Daniel Pinchbeck. In non-Beat matters, David Halberstam's *The Fifties* (New York: Villard, 1993) retailed the sweeping trends of the period.

Neal Cassady described his patrimony in *The First Third* (San Francisco: City Lights, 1971). Bob Dylan praised *On the Road* in *Chronicles Volume One* (New York: Simon & Schuster, 2004). The Tupac lyrics are from "Dear Mama," off *Me Against the World* (Jive, 1995). James Baldwin's comment on the lilac night scene comes from *Nobody Knows My Name* (New York: Dial Press, 1961), and Eldridge Cleaver's comes from *Soul on Ice* (New York: Dell, 1968). Leslie Fiedler threw down in *Waiting for the End* (New York: Stein and Day, 1964). Kenneth Rexroth scolded Kerouac in "The Voice of the Beat Generation Has Some Square Delusions," *San Francisco Chronicle*, February 16, 1958. Ann Douglas discussed Kerouac's "experiment in language" in "On the Road Again," in *The New York Times*, April 9, 1995, and Thelonious Monk in "Feel the City's Pulse? It's Be-bop, Man," in *The New York Times*, August 28, 1998. Armstrong's criticism of bop appears in Ted Gioia's *The History of Jazz* (New York: Oxford University Press, 1997).

Dana Heller and Elena Volkova discuss fools and Dostoyevsky in "The Holy Fool in Russian and American Culture: A Dialogue" (American Studies International, February 1, 2003, vol. 41, pp. 152–78). John Saward's *Perfect Fools: Folly for Christ's Sake in Catholic and Orthodox Spirituality* (Oxford: Oxford University Press, 1980) added to this book's share of foolishness, though I hold him blameless. Ginsberg's take on the critical backlash came from an interview in *Gargoyle* magazine, issue 10, by Eric Baizer, Reywas Divad and Richard Peabody. David Gates's Beat notes are at salon.com/books/feature/1999/04/12/beats/. The conservative Christian review of *On the Road* is from "The Path Less Beaten," by Stephen H. Webb, in *Touchstone* magazine, October, 2005. I think he nails it.

Finally, props to Tim Hunt's *Kerouac's Crooked Road: The Development of a Fiction* (Hamden, CT: Archon Books, 1981) for its analysis of the continuities between *On the Road* and *Visions of Cody*, and for his close reading of both texts. And if anyone truly cracks the meaning of the urinal scene, drop me a line.

ACKNOWLEDGMENTS

Many thanks to Paul Slovak for steady editorial guidance, and to my agent, Paul Bresnick, for both wisdom and encouragement. Bill Adler, John Capouya and Julia Hysell generously read the manuscript and gave valuable feedback. Jordan Leland prevented numerous errors from seeing print. I'm indebted to my *Times* colleagues, especially Suzanne Daley, Dana Canedy and Barbara Graustark, for allowing me breathing space to work on the book, and to John Sampas for permission to quote from unpublished Kerouac letters. Gary Stimeling copyedited the text. And as always, Risa and Jordan made it all worthwhile.